-Z
of Grammar
and **Punctuation**

Oxford **A-Z of Grammar** and **Punctuation**

John Seely

OXFORD
UNIVERSITY PRESS

OXFORD
UNIVERSITY PRESS

Great Clarendon Street, Oxford OX2 6DP

Oxford University Press is a department of the University of Oxford.
It furthers the University's objective of excellence in research, scholarship,
and education by publishing worldwide in

Oxford New York

Auckland Cape Town Dar es Salaam Hong Kong Karachi
Kuala Lumpur Madrid Melbourne Mexico City Nairobi
New Delhi Shanghai Taipei Toronto

With offices in

Argentina Austria Brazil Chile Czech Republic France Greece
Guatemala Hungary Italy Japan Poland Portugal Singapore
South Korea Switzerland Thailand Turkey Ukraine Vietnam

Oxford is a registered trade mark of Oxford University Press
in the UK and in certain other countries

Published in the United States
by Oxford University Press Inc., New York

© John Seely 2004, 2007, 2009

The moral rights of the author have been asserted
Database right Oxford University Press (maker)

First published 2004
Reissued with new cover 2007
Second edition 2009

British Library Cataloguing in Publication Data
Data available

Library of Congress Cataloging in Publication Data
Data available

Typeset by SPI Publisher Services, Pondicherry, India
Printed in Great Britain by Ashford Colour Press Ltd, Gosport, Hampshire

ISBN 978-0-19-956467-5

5 7 9 10 8 6 4

Contents

How this book is arranged

As the title implies, the main arrangement is alphabetical: there are just over 300 headwords, each of which provides a definition and/or explanation of a grammatical term. Headwords are shown by colour and font:

> **infinitive**

However, in a book of this kind, it is important to show the inter-relationships between different items. This is done in a number of ways.

Master headwords

As far as possible, headwords have been grouped together into families of related terms. So, for example, the following headwords have obvious links:

| absolute | attributive | classifying | comparative |
| grading | predicative | qualitative | superlative |

They all relate to **adjectives**, and the entry for that term provides an introduction to both adjectives and these related concepts. To indicate this, such master headwords are presented in a tinted box, like this:

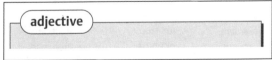

Cross references

Within all entries, cross references are indicated by the use of bold type. Master headwords occurring within the text are in blue:

> **infinitive**
>
> A form of the **verb**. In the **verb phrase** the infinitive

There are also explicit cross references:

> **Further information**
> See also: **phrasal verb**.

Diagrams

At the end of many of the master headword entries the information is summed up in a diagram, which also brings together many or all of the related terms:

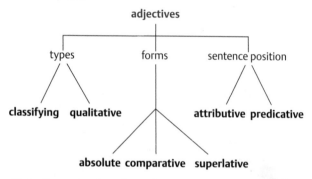

List of master headwords

abbreviation	dash	possession
adjective	determiner	preposition
adverb	exclamation	pronoun
adverbial	mark	pronunciation
agreement	full stop	punctuation
apostrophe	grammar	question mark
apposition	hyphen	semicolon
aspect	inverted	sentence
brackets	commas	slash
capital letters	mood	spelling
case	noun	tense
clause	paragraph	verb
colon	parenthesis	voice
comma	person	word
conjunction	phrase	word structure

Introduction to grammar

How English sentences work

This reference book is organized so that readers can find the terms they are looking for as quickly as possible. For this purpose an A-Z arrangement is the most suitable. The problem with grammar, however, is that in order to understand one term, you usually need to know what one or more other terms mean. For example, if you look up the term **abstract noun** the explanation assumes that you know what a **noun** is. If you look up **noun**, it takes it for granted that you know what a **phrase** is, and so on. Readers who have little or no background knowledge about grammar may find this very frustrating. So the purpose of this section is to provide a brief introduction to the basic terms of English grammar.

Types of sentence

We can use sentences for four main purposes in communication:

■ to make a statement:

   That car is travelling very fast.

■ to ask a question:

   Is that car breaking the speed limit?

■ to give an order or make a request:

   Don't drive so fast!

■ to make an exclamation:

   How fast that car is travelling!

Each has a different structure, but since statement sentences are by far the commonest, the explanations in this introduction concentrate on them.

Grammar levels

When we analyse how sentences work, we need to be able to look at a number of separate but related grammatical levels:

Introduction to grammar

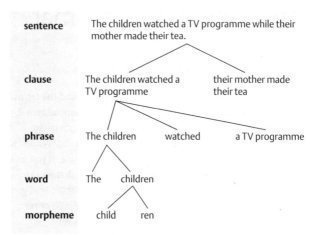

sentence	The children watched a TV programme while their mother made their tea.
clause	The children watched a TV programme / their mother made their tea
phrase	The children / watched / a TV programme
word	The / children
morpheme	child / ren

Clauses

The simplest sentences in English consist of just one **clause**. In the diagram above there are two clauses, each of which could stand alone as a sentence:

> The children watched a TV programme.

> Their mother made their tea.

A sentence can consist of one or more clauses. If it contains just one clause it is referred to as a simple sentence. If it contains more than one, then it is a multiple sentence. Multiple sentences can be **compound** or **complex**. These will be explained later in this introduction.

If you look at the two example clauses above, you can see that they follow a similar pattern. Each begins with words that indicate what the sentence is about:

> The children

> Their mother

This is the **subject** of the clause.

In each case the subject is followed by a word which refers to an action:

> watched

> made

This is the **verb** of the clause.

After the verb comes a group of words which provides information about the action of the verb. In each case they answer the question 'What?':

> – The children watched ...

> – What?

> – a TV programme.

These words after the verb form the **object** of the clause:

> a TV programme

> their tea

So our two sample clauses follow the pattern subject + verb + object. The subject, the verb, and the object are components of the clause, and 'subject + verb + object' is the pattern of the clause.

Clause components and patterns

Clauses can contain five different components:

■ subject

■ verb

■ object

■ complement

■ adverbial

Subject + verb

The simplest pattern for a clause is a subject followed by a verb. The subject tells us what the sentence is about and the verb tells us what the subject is doing, or has been doing:

SUBJECT	OBJECT
Birds	sing.
A very large and ugly chicken	was squawking.

Subject + verb + object

If there is an object, it normally follows the verb. It refers to a different person or thing from the subject. Frequently that person or thing is affected by the action described by the verb:

SUBJECT	VERB	OBJECT
Mary	writes	books.

Subject + verb + complement

A small number of verbs are followed not by an object, but by a complement. The commonest of these verbs is 'be'. For example:

SUBJECT	VERB	COMPLEMENT
Mary	is	a writer.

In clauses like this the verb acts like an equal sign:

Mary = a writer

Subject + verb + object + complement

It is also possible to have part of a clause that completes the object:

SUBJECT	VERB	OBJECT	COMPLEMENT
The company	made	him	CEO.

In these sentences the imaginary equal sign is between the object and its complement:

The company made him = CEO.

Subject + verb + object + object

A number of verbs can have not just one but two objects. In the sentence *Miriam gave her brother a present* both *her brother* and *a present* are objects, but in different ways. The two objects answer different questions:

- What did Miriam give?

- A present.

- Whom did she give it to?

- Her brother.

A present is called the **direct object** and *her brother* the **indirect object**.

SUBJECT	VERB	INDIRECT OBJECT	DIRECT OBJECT
Miriam	gave	her brother	a present.

This gives us five common clause patterns:

- **subject** + **verb**

    Birds sing.

- **subject** + **verb** + **object**

    Mary writes books.

- **subject** + **verb** + **complement**

    Mary is a writer.

- **subject** + **verb** + **object** + **complement**

    The company made him CEO.

- **subject** + **verb** + **indirect object** + **direct object**

    Miriam gave her brother a present.

In each of these patterns each component, subject, verb, etc. is essential; if you remove any of them, you destroy the grammar of the clause and make the sentence either meaningless or difficult to untangle.

Adverbials

There remains one clause component that is much less straightforward: adverbials. These are words or phrases that answer questions such as:

- Where?

    here   down the road

- When?

  later   after a few hours

- How?

  slowly   with great difficulty

- Why?

  for the sake of the children   because of the bad weather

In a small number of clauses an adverbial is an essential component, just like a verb or an object; it is required by the type of verb used:

- subject + verb + adverbial

  They have been living on their savings.

- subject + verb + object + adverbial

  I placed the book on the table.

If you remove the adverbial from these clauses you destroy their grammar and leave questions unanswered:

  – They have been living ...

  – How?

  – on their savings.

Optional adverbials

More often an adverbial is not essential to the grammar of the clause it is in. In each of the sentences that follow the adverbial is in bold type.

  He found a secret passage **behind the fireplace**.

  She is **usually** a very happy child.

  Last week Mr and Mrs Holt came to see us.

In each case if you remove the adverbial the clause is still grammatical and still makes sense. As the examples show, adverbials can occur in different positions in the clause. Sometimes they can be moved to a different position:

  He found a secret passage **behind the fireplace**.

  Behind the fireplace he found a secret passage.

This does not mean that they can be placed anywhere in the clause. The following arrangement is impossible:

He **behind the fireplace** found a secret passage.

Simple and multiple sentences

If a sentence consists of one clause it is described as a simple sentence. Each of the following is a simple sentence:

Mary writes books.

She has not been very successful.

She is looking for another career.

If a sentence contains more than one clause it is described as a multiple sentence. Each of the following sentences is multiple:

She has not been very successful and she is looking for another career.

Although Mary writes books, she has not been very successful.

Compound sentences

Multiple sentences are made by combining clauses. The simplest way of doing this is to use the grammatical equivalent of a plus sign:

| She has not been very successful | + | she is looking for another career. |

The commonest words to do this job are:

and   but   or

It is possible to string together as many clauses as you like in this way:

She has not been very successful **and** she is looking for another career, **but** so far she has not had much luck **and** has decided to try a different tack **or** even give up altogether, **but** ...

until your readers either get lost or give up in disgust!

Complex sentences

There is a limit to the meaning you can express with the conjunction *and*. If someone says *She has not been very successful and she is looking for another career*, we can probably work out that looking for another career is a result of not being very successful, but sometimes joining two clauses by *and* can leave the connection between them very unclear:

> The new CEO was appointed and Martin resigned.

This sentence describes two events but it doesn't show what connection there was between them—always supposing there was any connection at all. We could link the two clauses in ways that *did* show a connection. For example:

> **Before** the new CEO was appointed Martin resigned.

> **After** the new CEO was appointed Martin resigned.

> **Although** the new CEO was appointed Martin resigned.

> The new CEO was appointed **so** Martin resigned.

In compound sentences the clauses joined together are of equal status; we can cut the sentence up into clauses and each of them will become an independent simple sentence. Complex sentences work in a different way. One of the clauses is the main clause and the others are subordinate to it. The subordinate clauses form a single component of the main clause: subject, object, complement, or adverbial. In the first of each of the pairs of sentences that follow the subordinate clause is in bold type. In the second sentence it has been replaced by a word or short phrase.

■ **subject**

> **What you did yesterday** was inexcusable.

> **It** was inexcusable.

■ **object**

> I cannot forgive **what you did yesterday**.

> I cannot forgive **your action**.

■ **complement**

> That is **what I admire about Billie**.

> That is **it**.

Introduction to grammar

■ **adverbial**

> **After the new CEO was appointed** Martin resigned.

> **Afterwards** Martin resigned.

Phrases

The first clause pattern introduced was this:

SUBJECT	OBJECT
Birds	sing.
A very large and ugly **chicken**	was **squawking**.

As you can see from the example sentences, sometimes the subject or object may be a single word (e.g. *Birds*) and at others it is a group of words (e.g. *A very large and ugly chicken*). In grammar, groups of words that form part of a sentence pattern are called **phrases**.

A phrase is a group of words built upon a single word. In the examples above, that single word, or **headword**, is printed in bold type. If the headword is a noun, then the phrase is called a **noun phrase**. *A very large and ugly chicken* is a noun phrase: *was squawking* is a verb phrase. Another very common type of phrase is the **prepositional phrase**. Prepositional phrases always begin with a preposition. Prepositions are words placed before a noun or a noun phrase and they give information about position, time, and other things. Examples are:

> in   at   up   before

Examples of prepositional phrases are:

> in the garden

> over my dead body

> for several hours

Words and morphemes

So far we have looked at four grammatical levels: sentence, clause, phrase, word. There is just one more we need to be aware of. Some words can change their form depending on where they are placed in a sentence and how they are used. For example, nouns change their form according to whether they are singular or plural:

house – houses

child – children

Each of these plurals consists of two parts:

house + s

child + ren

Each part conveys meaning: *house* refers to a familiar type of building, while -*s* indicates that there is more than one. These parts are referred to as **morphemes**.

We can analyse verb forms in a similar way. For example, the verb forms *walk/walks/walking/walked* consist of the morphemes *walk/s/ing/ed*.

Some personal pronouns have different forms according to whether they are the subject or the object of the sentence:

He was my boss at Sanders & Webb.

I couldn't stand **him**.

These, too, are morphemes. The study of how words change their forms according to use is referred to as **morphology**.

abbreviation

The presentation of abbreviations in writing raises two
questions:

■ Should I use full stops?

■ Do I use capital or small letters?

Full stops

Normally if you use initial (first) letters to represent words
there is no need to put a full stop after them:

UK   BBC

In North America, however, it is more common to use a full stop
(or 'period') after initial letters.

If the abbreviation consists of the first and last letters of the
word, then you do not use a full stop:

Mr   Ltd

If the abbreviation consists of the first part of a word, then you
put a full stop at the end:

Wed.   Dec.

Capital or small letters

Normally if you use the first letter of a word in an abbreviation,
then a capital letter is used:

HND   BAA   HSBC

One well-known exception to this rule is the abbreviation *plc* for
public limited company, although this is also sometimes written
PLC.

See also: **acronym.**

absolute

Many **adjectives** have three forms:

ABSOLUTE	COMPARATIVE	SUPERLATIVE
big	bigger	biggest
certain	more certain	most certain

a

We use the **comparative** when two items are being compared:

The rabbit was **bigger** than the cat.

The **superlative** is used when there are more than two:

The Mandela Theatre is the **biggest** of the three.

The absolute form is used when a plain statement is being made without any kind of comparison:

Patchwork is **big** again this year.

abstract noun

Nouns can be divided into two groups: concrete and abstract. Concrete nouns refer to people, places, and things that can be experienced using our five senses. Abstract nouns refer to thoughts, ideas, and imaginings that cannot:

CONCRETE	ABSTRACT
man	manliness
table	tabulation
author	authorship

Too many obscure abstractions can make a piece of writing difficult to read. For example the sentence in bold type in the following extract:

Such people may be keen to work, but unable to find jobs because none are available in their occupation or in their geographical area, so that re-training or re-housing would be necessary to increase the chances of employment. **It could also be that there is a general deficiency of demand for labour throughout the economy, in which case the involuntarily unemployed workers will face fierce competition for the jobs that do become available**.

A general deficiency of demand for labour throughout the economy is just a pompous and long-winded way of saying that there aren't enough jobs to go round. On the other hand there are also many everyday abstract nouns that are simple and direct:

happiness   failure   truth   beauty

It would be perverse to try to avoid abstract nouns such as these, so the use of abstract nouns in writing is a question of judgement.

accent

'Accent' is often used to describe pronunciation which the speaker considers different from 'normal':

> His intonation and emphasis were all wrong, some of the articles got switched, and he had a noticeable **accent** when speaking in English.

Often what people mean is that a speaker is using the pronunciation that is typical of a particular region of Britain, America, or elsewhere:

> I was bullied because I had an unusual surname and a broad Liverpudlian **accent**.

In fact, everyone has an accent: it is simply the way in which each individual pronounces English words. It is most strongly marked in the way different **vowels** are sounded. For example, the vowels in 'bath' and 'bun' are pronounced differently in the north and south of England.

Accent should not be confused with **dialect**. While accent concerns only the pronunciation of the language, dialect is concerned with vocabulary (**lexis**) and **grammar**.

acronym

An abbreviation composed of the first letters of other words so that the abbreviation itself forms a word. For example:

> CRASSH: Centre for Research in the Arts, Social Sciences and Humanities

> Aids: acquired immune deficiency syndrome

Acronyms are treated just like ordinary words in a sentence, and may be composed of all capital letters, or of an initial capital followed by small letters. For example:

> His policy on Aids has earned him some international praise.

active voice

Transitive verbs (verbs that take an **object**) can be used in two ways, or 'voices': active and passive.

> **Active:** The dog bit him.

> **passive:** He was bitten by the dog.

a

Transitive verbs usually describe some kind of action. In the sentence *The dog bit him*, you have a person, thing, or idea that performs the action and one that is affected by it. The first is the **subject** *The dog*, and the second the **object** *him*. When we put a sentence into the passive voice, the object *him* becomes the subject *He*. The original subject *The dog* becomes the agent and has the **preposition** *by* placed in front of it. This changes the emphasis of the sentence considerably.

In everyday writing the active voice is much more common than the passive.

See also: **passive voice**; **voice**.

addresses

Styles for the presentation of addresses in letters and on envelopes have changed over the years. Contemporary practice is to set addresses with the left hand end of lines square ('left justified') and without any punctuation:

Oxford University Press
Great Clarendon Street
OXFORD
OX2 6DP

The British Post Office recommend that the town or city is in block capitals. The postcode is placed separately, on a line of its own, except in the case of London addresses, where it is still conventionally placed on the same line as London:

LONDON WC1 6GE

Forms of address

The commonest titles used in addresses are:

Miss   Mr   Mrs   Ms

Mr and *Mrs* are straightforward to use. *Mr* is used for all men who have no other title, while *Mrs* is used for married women. Women who are not married can be addressed in letters as *Miss*, but some women prefer *Ms*. A number of married women also prefer to be addressed as *Ms*. If you are in a situation where you do not know the preferences of the person you are writing to, then it is safest to use *Mrs* for married women and *Ms* for unmarried women.

The commonest professional title is *Dr* for doctors (both medical practitioners and those who have a higher university degree). Members of the clergy are addressed as *The Reverend* (abbreviated to *Revd*).

See also: **abbreviation**; **capital letters**; **full stop**.

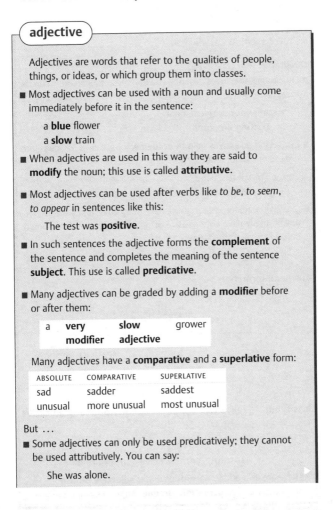

adjective

Adjectives are words that refer to the qualities of people, things, or ideas, or which group them into classes.

■ Most adjectives can be used with a noun and usually come immediately before it in the sentence:

a **blue** flower
a **slow** train

■ When adjectives are used in this way they are said to **modify** the noun; this use is called **attributive**.

■ Most adjectives can be used after verbs like *to be*, *to seem*, *to appear* in sentences like this:

The test was **positive**.

■ In such sentences the adjective forms the **complement** of the sentence and completes the meaning of the sentence **subject**. This use is called **predicative**.

■ Many adjectives can be graded by adding a **modifier** before or after them:

a	**very**	**slow**	grower
	modifier	**adjective**	

Many adjectives have a **comparative** and a **superlative** form:

ABSOLUTE	COMPARATIVE	SUPERLATIVE
sad	sadder	saddest
unusual	more unusual	most unusual

But ...

■ Some adjectives can only be used predicatively; they cannot be used attributively. You can say:

She was **alone**.

but you cannot say:

> I saw an alone woman. ✗

- Some adjectives can only be used attributively; they cannot be used predicatively. You can say:

> It was a mere skirmish.

but you cannot say:

> The skirmish was mere. ✗

Qualitative and classifying

- Qualitative adjectives describe the qualities of a person, thing, or idea. For example:

> a **stupendous** achievement
> an **exciting** proposal

- Classifying adjectives help to divide persons, things, or ideas into groups or classes. For example:

> the **French** language
> an **annual** event

- Classifying adjectives cannot usually be **graded** and they do not normally have comparative or superlative forms. So it would be odd to say, for example:

> It was a very annual event. ✗

Further information

More information and examples will be found as follows:

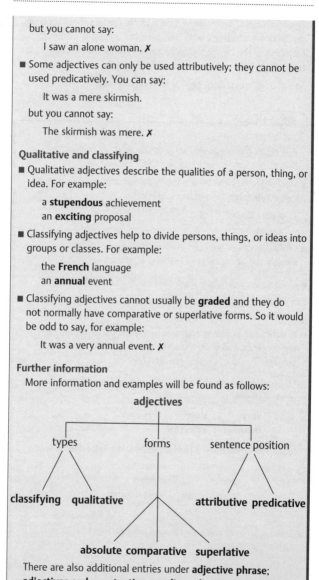

There are also additional entries under **adjective phrase**; **adjectives and punctuation**; **grading adjectives**; and **unique**.

adjective phrase

An adjective phrase is a group of words built up on an **adjective**. There are two main ways in which this is done.

■ An adverb is placed in front of the adjective:

'He's a	very	remarkable	man,' said Alison.
	adverb	adjective	
	adjective phrase		

The adverb modifies the adjective by changing its meaning. *Very* is the commonest adverb used in this way. Others are:

    rather   quite   fairly

You can have more than one adverb in front of the adjective. For example:

    I'm **really rather** busy at the moment.

■ Sometimes words are placed after the adjective to modify it in a similar way:

ADJECTIVE	MODIFIER(S)
slow	enough
easy	enough to spot

adjectives and punctuation

When two or more adjectives are used in a list the question arises: should they be separated by commas? There are no clear-cut rules about this but the following guidelines may help.

■ No comma is needed to separate adjectives of different types, e.g. a qualitative and a classifying adjective:

    a **large Spanish** bank

■ Use a comma between two or more qualitative adjectives:

    long, slender legs

a

■ If the adjectives are all classifying adjectives, use commas if they all relate to the same class of information:

English, French, and Spanish editions

but not if they don't:

the **French nuclear** reactor

adjunct

Adjuncts are **adverbials** that add more information to a sentence. They can provide additional information about:

■ **cause**

They just get into crime **because of the lack of other options**.

■ **concession**

Some producers abandoned their oak barrels in favour of stainless steel, which, **although expensive**, is very much easier to use.

■ **condition**

As soon as the dormant plants arrive, open the packages and, **if necessary**, moisten the roots.

■ **manner**

Jonathan's mind was working **at top speed** …

■ **place**

… a fifth of our kids live **below the poverty line** …

■ **purpose**

This is not for reasons of sympathy to the criminal, but **in the interests of the society to which he will return**.

■ **result**

In mid-December the UN mission again pleaded for funds for teachers, police officers, and other civil servants, **to little effect**.

■ **time**

Eisler was obliged to leave Germany, and **after various travels** arrived in New York **in 1938**.

adverb

Adverbs make up a **word class** or 'part of speech'. They have two main uses.

As adverbials
They are often used as **adverbials**, providing information about, for example, place, time, and manner:

- **place**

  here   away   somewhere

- **time**

  soon   already   still

- **manner**

  easily   fast   slowly

When they are used in this way they are also referred to as **adjuncts**.

They can also be used as **sentence adverbials**. These are of two types:

- **conjuncts**, which link sentences within a text:

  First off they have to be original issue to be considered a true classic. **Secondly**, they should be in good nick, preferably still unworn, with the box intact.

- **disjuncts**, which allow the speaker to comment on the text:

  Unfortunately, this great book is no longer in print.

As modifiers
Adverbs can also be used to **modify adjectives** and thus form **adjective phrases**:

ADVERB	ADJECTIVE
very	easy
rather	attractive

a

They can work in a similar way with other adverbs to make **adverb phrases**:

ADVERB	ADVERB
quite	soon
extremely	slowly

Further information

The information above is summed up in the diagram below. Each of the words in bold type has its own entry, where further information can be found.

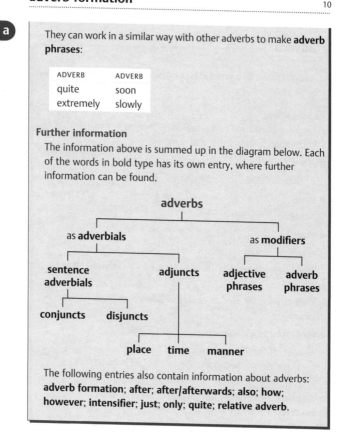

The following entries also contain information about adverbs: **adverb formation**; **after**; **after/afterwards**; **also**; **how**; **however**; **intensifier**; **just**; **only**; **quite**; **relative adverb**.

adverb formation

Many adverbs are formed from adjectives by adding *-ly*:

slow + ly → slowly

Rules

■ The base rule is that you add *-ly* to the adjective:

sad → sadly

a

■ If the adjective ends in –*ll*, just add –*y*.

    full → fully

■ Most adjectives of one syllable that end in –*y* are regular, with the exception of *gay* → *gaily*, *dry* → *drily* or *dryly*, *sly* → *slyly* or *slily*.

■ For two-syllable adjectives that end in –*y*, replace the final *y* with the letters *ily*:

    happy → happily

■ For adjectives that end with a consonant followed by –*le*, replace the final *e* with *y*:

    terrible → terribly

Adjectives that end in –*ly* cannot be transformed by adding –*ly*. Instead, use a short phrase:

    friendly → in a friendly way

adverbial

Function

An adverbial is a single word or a group of words that forms part of a clause. There are three types of adverbial:

■ **adjuncts**. These provide additional information.
For example:

> It is safe to climb up or down either path **at walking pace**.

Adjuncts can provide information about:

cause	**concession**	**condition**	**manner**
place	**purpose**	**result**	**time**

■ **conjuncts**. These provide a link between sentences:

> It appears that previews for *Billy Elliot: The Musical* have been postponed due to fear for the health of the many child actors. Three child actors rotate the title role. **In addition**, there are 45 other child actors involved in the production.

■ **disjuncts**. You use these to make your own comments on the information you are communicating:

▶

Unfortunately it is unlikely that your boss will change his ways.

Form

An adverbial can be one of the following:

- an **adverb**

  In *Unforgiven*, Eastwood plays a mercenary who is **reluctantly** drawn back into the game of murder and revenge …

- an **adverb phrase**

  It is also the case that the BBC performs **rather poorly** when it is most concerned about ratings …

- a **prepositional phrase**

  So, **under the guise of time off for research**, many university faculty spend their working day elsewhere at other jobs, neither reading nor writing new material.

- a **noun phrase**

  I'll ask them **next week** when we rehearse for the new album.

Further information

The information given above is summed up in the diagram below. Each of the words in bold type has its own entry, where further information can be found.

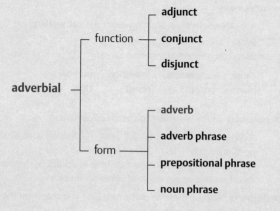

The following entries also contain information about adverbials:
adverbial position; focus; sentence adverbial.

a

adverbial clause

A clause in a **complex sentence** which provides **adverbial** information about:

■ **cause**

> **Because it was cold**, there were goose bumps on her arm.

■ **concession**

> Clare has seen it, **although she probably hasn't had time to read it fully**.

■ **condition**

> **If you see a stranger acting suspiciously outside your home or your neighbour's** call the police.

■ **manner**

> Jamison had come by to run a check of the medical monitor **as he always did before a dive**.

■ **place**

> **Where the river straightened**, he took his chance to check the barometer.

■ **purpose**

> They joined a major label **so that they could sell records throughout the world**.

■ **result**

> This was written so quickly **that several errors occurred**.

■ **time**

> **When dawn broke**, the rain ceased and the various parties were able to take stock of their positions.

a

adverbial position

Beginning or end

An **adverbial** can come at the beginning or end of a **clause** or **sentence**. For example:

> **After several hours of random identity checks**, the troops dispersed.

> The troops dispersed **after several hours of random identity checks**.

This does not mean that all adverbials can take both positions. For example, while you can say:

> The trees rushed past **at great speed**.

you cannot say:

> **At great speed** the trees rushed past.

This is because the adverbial *at great speed* refers particularly to the action described by the verb *rushed*, and this link is destroyed if you separate it from the verb.

Middle

Adverbials can also be placed in the middle of the sentence. This is particularly true of single word adverbials (**adverbs**). The key to placing the adverbial correctly is the **verb**. If the verb consists of a single word, then the adverbial is usually placed immediately before it:

> They **finally** reached the deck.

If there is an **auxiliary verb** and a **main verb** the adverbial is placed between them:

They	have	finally	reached	the deck.
	auxiliary verb	**adverbial**	**main verb**	

In such sentences, adverbials cannot be placed between the main verb and its object or complement:

> They have reached **finally** the deck. ✗

adverb phrase

A group of words built up round an **adverb** by adding words before and/or after it. For example:

	adverb	
very	smoothly	
as	economically	as possible

after

This word commonly refers to time, helping us to explain the order in which events happen:

> She went back to work very quickly **after** her operation.

It can also sometimes refer to space, usually helping place objects in order:

> 'Where are you going?' said Lee, coming **after** him.

After can be:

■ a **preposition**

> **After** his election Dr Kumar spoke of the racial attacks he endured during the campaign.

■ a **subordinating conjunction**

> **After** he was elected in November, he revealed that he had been the subject of racial attacks during his campaign.

■ an **adverb**

> Then he spun around and strode out of the door, his men following **after** without a word.

It is also used to **modify** a **noun** in **phrases** such as *the morning after*.

after/afterwards

In formal writing, *after* should not be used as an adverb of time. Instead use *afterwards*:

> It was not so easy to brush him off **afterwards**. ✓

not

a

It was not so easy to brush him off **after**. ✗

The exception to this is when it follows a word or phrase giving a measure of time. For example:

But what about the year **after**? ✓

---

agreement

The **subject** and the **verb** of a **clause** have to agree in **number** and **person**.

PERSON	NUMBER	PRONOUN(S)	TO WRITE	TO BE
1st	singular	I	write	am
1st	plural	we	write	are
2nd	singular	you	write	are
		(thou)	(writest)	(art)
2nd	plural	you	write	are
3rd	singular	he, she, it	writes	is
3rd	plural	they	write	are

Writers sometimes fail to make the verb of a sentence agree with the subject. This usually happens when the subject of the sentence is a lengthy **noun phrase**. For example:

The advent of digitization and electronic media **make** speedy cooperation between us even more necessary. ✗

This should be:

The advent of digitization and electronic media **makes** speedy cooperation between us even more necessary. ✓

The rule is that the verb should agree with the main word in the subject, the **headword** of the phrase. If in doubt, you should try to reduce the subject to a single **noun** or **pronoun**. In this case the subject boils down to *advent*, which is singular.

---

also

This is an adverb, used to link items in a sentence or to make links between sentences. For example:

The oxygen they produce benefits the fish, and they **also** provide a source of food and shelter.

It is frequently used with *and* or *but*, but it is not a conjunction. In formal writing *also* should not be used instead of *and*:

The closet is larger than a pit and therefore lasts longer **also** it is easy to empty. ✗

Here the speaker needs to add *and* (→ *and also*), or replace *also* with *and*.

and

A **coordinating conjunction** which is used to join two items. These can be:

■ two **words**

bread **and** butter

to **and** fro

■ two **phrases**

eight European countries **and** a number of international agencies

■ two **clauses**

Then he rolled off the seat into the footwell **and** immediately started snoring again.

antonym

A word meaning the opposite of another word. For example, the following are pairs of antonyms:

wet	dry
buy	sell
child	adult

any

A word that can be used in these ways:

■ **determiner**

I sat in my cell, expecting to be called out for execution at **any** moment.

a

■ **pronoun**

I don't think there'll be **any** to spare for a day or two.

■ **adverb**

It can be used before the **comparative** form of an **adjective** or **adverb**. For example:

Why won't the car go **any** faster?

---

apostrophe

The apostrophe is the punctuation mark which causes more people more problems than any other. It is used for two purposes:

1. To show that one or more letters have been missed out

When we are speaking, we frequently elide certain sounds, running parts of a word together. For example *did not* becomes *didn't*. When these words are written down, an apostrophe is used to show that letters have been missed out:

will not	→	won't
shall not	→	shan't
might have	→	might've
she is	→	she's
they are	→	they're

As the examples show, the way in which some of these shortened forms are written down is rather selective. It works well when *is* and *are* are shortened, but in the case of *won't* and *shan't*, the apostrophe does not show where all the letters have been omitted; otherwise we would write *sha'n't* (✗), and no rule can cover the change from *will not* to *won't*.

2. To show possession

We also use the apostrophe to show that something belongs to someone. For example:

Lord Rochester's monkey
the girl's handbag
the Browns' Silver Wedding anniversary
the churches' position on gay priests

▶

The rules are:

■ If the name or noun is in the singular, we add an apostrophe followed by the letter *s*.

■ If the name or noun is a plural ending in *s* then we simply add an apostrophe.

■ Plurals that do not end in *s* follow the rule for singular nouns:
     a children's playground

■ There is one exception to these rules. When *its* means 'of it' there is no apostrophe.

apposition

Placing one **noun** or **noun phrase** next to another in a sentence so that it explains or amplifies it. For example:

The writer Michael Viney left Dublin 13 years ago to live a life of peace and self-sufficiency in a remote house.

Here the short phrases *the writer* and *Michael Viney* work in parallel. They are said to be in **apposition** to each other.

In the example above, the sentence would work grammatically with only one of the phrases:

The writer left Dublin 13 years ago to live a life of peace and self-sufficiency in a remote house.

Michael Viney left Dublin 13 years ago to live a life of peace and self-sufficiency in a remote house.

But neither of these alternative versions is very satisfactory. The first leads us to ask, 'Which writer?', while the second prompts: 'Who is Michael Viney?'

article

A word class from traditional grammar. It consists of these words:

a

- *a, an* indefinite article
- *the* definite article

Articles form part of a larger class of words known as **determiners**.

as

A word that can be used in three main ways:

Subordinating conjunction

It can introduce a number of different types of **adverbial clause**:

- **time**

    As the train drew into Victoria station, Gloria softened.

- **cause**

    As they are fast-drying ... the application technique is slightly different.

- **manner**

    The talk that night was about experiments carried out to explain why people behaved **as** they did.

The first two of these uses are commoner than the last; in them *as* can mean 'while' or 'because'. Occasionally this can cause confusion if a sentence is carelessly constructed. For example:

I left the farm **as** it was getting late.

Does this mean when it was getting late, or because it was getting late?

Preposition

As can also be used as a **preposition**:

Should I get a job **as** a barmaid?

Adverb

It can also be used as an **adverb** in comparisons:

He's **as** happy **as** a sandboy.

aspect

The form of the verb phrase provides information about the speaker's attitude towards the action s/he is describing. There are three aspects: ▶

■ **simple**

> I work.
>
> ... I **work** half an hour up the road from my house ...

■ **continuous**

> I am working.
>
> I already have an idea that I **am working** on ...

■ **perfect**

> I have worked.
>
> ... I **have worked** in India and I still do ...

As these examples show, while the simple aspect just uses the **main verb**, the continuous aspect requires the **auxiliary verb** *be*, and the perfect requires the auxiliary *have*.

More information and examples will be found as follows:

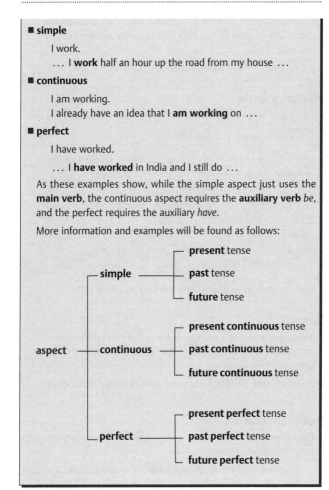

attributive

The attributive use of an **adjective** is when the adjective modifies a **noun**. For example:

> ... a **brilliant metallic-green-coloured oval** insect ...

This is contrasted with the **predicative** use, when the adjective comes after a **verb** such as *to be* and forms the **complement** of the sentence:

My closest friend was **brilliant**.

auxiliary verb

A group of **verbs** that combine with the **main verb** to form the verb phrase:

		is	am	are	was	were	been
PRIMARY	be						
	have	has			had		
	do	does			did		done
	shall	will	should	would			
	can		could				
MODAL	may		might				
	must						
	ought (to)						

See also: **modal auxiliary verb**; **primary auxiliary verb**.

base

The word or part of a word to which prefixes and suffixes are attached to form new words. In the words that follow, the base is printed in bold type.

counter**act** under**achieve**ment un**necessari**ly un**happi**ness

both … and …

Coordinating conjunctions that can be used to link words, phrases, and, sometimes, clauses:

It's a rare movie that can look **both** cheap **and** costly at the same time.

A number of points should be remembered:

■ *Both* can only be used with two items, so it is wrong to say:

That can be both college, independent, and mainstream. ✗

brackets

b

- The two items to be joined must be grammatically equivalent, so it would be incorrect to write:

    It has to be both sincere and there's got to be some quality to the aesthetics of the music. ✗

Instead you should write:

    It has both to be sincere and to have some quality to the aesthetics of the music. ✓

- It is important to get *both* in the right place. Here it is not:

    Those combines may have a harmful effect both as regards public interests and those of the State. ✗

This should be:

    Those combines may have a harmful effect as regards both public interests and those of the State. ✓

---

brackets

A pair of punctuation marks used to indicate that the words enclosed are not essential to the meaning of the sentence, but provide additional information:

    What has been closed down at CERN is the LEP **(Large Electron Positron Collider)** accelerator, and you're right, so that in five years' time they will build the big LHC **(Large Hadron Collider)** inside there.

The words enclosed in brackets are described as being in **parenthesis**.

Brackets can be used to enclose additional information that doesn't fit into the grammatical structure of the sentence. For example:

    It's like any group of people **(virtual or in real life)**; you're going to have individuals who feel a certain way about an issue ...

Brackets are also used by some writers to make asides, comments to the reader which do not form part of the main argument or story being expressed. For example:

    This is also known as junk email ... or spam. Obviously, it's impossible to distribute processed lunchmeat electronically at this time **(and hopefully it'll never happen)**.

> In informal writing this is intended to make readers feel that the writer is talking directly to them, and it can be effective. But if it is used too much, it quickly becomes irritating.

but

A **coordinating conjunction** used to link together:

■ two words

tired **but** happy

■ two **phrases**

nice to look at **but** difficult to describe

■ two **clauses**

It's a very simple ceremony **but** it's really touching.

can

A **modal auxiliary verb**. It has two meanings:

■ that someone or something has the ability to do something:

Those who **can** swim, swim.

■ that something is possible:

I suppose anything **can** happen now.

can/may

can

Traditionally *can* is used to show:

■ ability

An English person who **can** speak even one other language fluently is rare.

■ possibility

Relapse **can** occur at any time.

may

This is normally used to show:

■ permission

Candidates **may** enter for both examinations, if desired.

■ possibility

It **may** cause pain, but often there are no symptoms.

Today *can* is increasingly used to show permission:

Mum, **can** I leave it?

Using *can* in this way is generally accepted, although many people still use *may* in more formal situations.

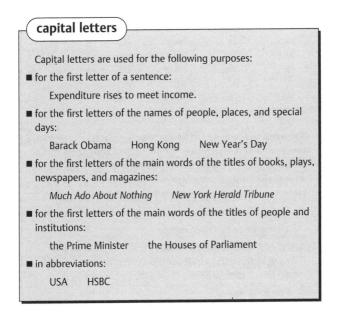

capital letters

Capital letters are used for the following purposes:

■ for the first letter of a sentence:

Expenditure rises to meet income.

■ for the first letters of the names of people, places, and special days:

Barack Obama   Hong Kong   New Year's Day

■ for the first letters of the main words of the titles of books, plays, newspapers, and magazines:

Much Ado About Nothing   *New York Herald Tribune*

■ for the first letters of the main words of the titles of people and institutions:

the Prime Minister   the Houses of Parliament

■ in abbreviations:

USA   HSBC

cardinal

See **numeral**.

case

Nouns and **pronouns** can be used as the **subject** or **object** of a sentence:

SUBJECT	VERB	OBJECT
The dog	bit	her.
She	sold	her dog.

As can be seen from this example, the pronoun *she* is used as the subject, but if it is used as the object it becomes *her*. These different forms are called cases. There are three cases in English, subjective, objective, and possessive:

SUBJECTIVE	OBJECTIVE	POSSESSIVE PRONOUN	POSSESSIVE DETERMINER
I	me	mine	my
we	us	ours	our
she	her	hers	her
he	him	his	his
it	it	its	its
you	you	yours	your
they	them	theirs	their

The subjective form is used for the subject of a **clause** or **sentence** and also, in formal language, for the **subject complement** (for example: *It is I*). The objective form is used for the object and also after **prepositions** (for example: *The person to whom I gave a present . . .*). The possessive forms are used in sentences such as:

England is **mine**. It owes me a living.

It's **my** job to be entertaining.

Nouns also have a possessive case. We add an **apostrophe** followed by the letter *s* to show this in singular nouns and add a simple apostrophe to plurals ending in *s*:

a person's name

my parents' Silver Wedding.

cause

Adverbials can be used to provide information about *why* something happened:

> She laughingly recalled a day when Pearl, then in her thirties, had **inexplicably** rolled a large rock into the living room of the house where she and other children were playing.

> The manure must not be treated **because of the potential harm to beneficial insects**.

Adverbial clauses can also be used to carry information about cause:

> It must has been pretty far back **since he could barely hear the sound of the waterfall**.

classifying adjective

An **adjective** that places the **noun** which it **modifies** into a group, class, or category. Examples of classifying adjectives are:

annual	Australian	female
military	nuclear	numerical

The other main group of adjectives is **qualitative adjectives**, which provide information about the qualities of a person, thing, or idea. Examples of qualitative adjectives are:

complicated	green	helpful
hot	loud	rapid

Classifying adjectives cannot usually be graded and they do not normally have comparative or superlative forms. So it would be odd to say, for example:

> It was a **very annual** event. ✗

clause

Sentences can consist of one or more clauses. Their part in grammatical structure is shown in this diagram:

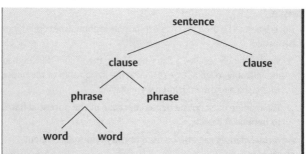

Clause structure

Clauses are made up of two or more clause components:

■ **subject**

■ **verb**

■ **object**

■ **complement**

■ **adverbial**.

All clauses used to make a statement normally contain a subject and a verb, in that order. They may also contain one or more additional components. All English clauses are based on one of seven basic patterns:

1	**subject**	**verb**		
	The sun	rose.		
2	**subject**	**verb**	**complement**	
	The light	was	low.	
3	**subject**	**verb**	**adverbial**	
	It	came	from the east.	
4	**subject**	**verb**	**object**	
	He	saw	the dawn.	
5	**subject**	**verb**	**object**	**object**
	He	gave	the dog	a bone.
6	**subject**	**verb**	**object**	**adverbial**
	It	took	it	away.
7	**subject**	**verb**	**object**	**complement**
	This	made	him	happy.

Clauses can be finite or **non-finite**. All the examples above are finite clauses.

How clauses are used

A sentence contains one or more clauses, which can be of one of two types:

■ main clause

A **simple sentence** consists of just one main clause:

Life is good.

A **compound sentence** contains two or more main clauses:

Kevin thought for a moment,	and then	he sprang forward.
main clause		**main clause**

A **complex sentence** contains one main clause and one or more subordinate clauses:

You're just saying that	because	you don't like Ellie.
main clause		**subordinate clause**

Here the subordinate clause is an **adverbial** of **cause.**

■ subordinate clause

In a complex sentence, a subordinate clause can act as the subject, object, complement, or adverbial of the main clause. In the sentences that follow, the subordinate clause is printed in bold and its function within the sentence is shown in brackets:

What Anthony did was an accident. (subject)

She also noticed **that the crew was not present**. (object)

That was **what first set me on his case**. (subject complement)

I was alone mainly **because everyone else was busy**. (adverbial)

Further information

The information given above is summed up in the diagram below. Each of the words in bold type has its own entry, where further information can be found. Words in blue have more extensive entries.

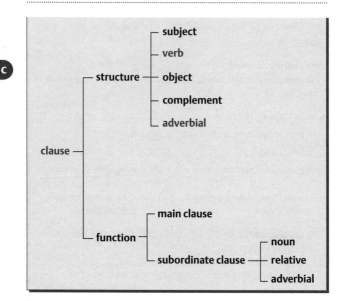

coherence

If you write more than one or two sentences on a subject, you have to ensure that your text holds together and makes sense to your readers. You do this by making sure that it has two important qualities:

- coherence
- cohesion

Coherence means that the thought behind the text is consistent and moves logically from one point to the next. A coherent text uses suitable vocabulary and uses it consistently.

cohesion

The use of grammatical devices to make sure that a text sticks together. The commonest of these are:

- **reference**
- **ellipsis**
- **sentence adverbials**.

collective noun

A **singular noun** that refers to several individuals. For example:

the police   the choir   Parliament

The main question raised by collective nouns is agreement: do you use a singular or a plural verb? Is it *the jury is …* or *the jury are …*? The answer is: it depends on the context. If the speaker is thinking of the jury as a united body, then the singular is used:

The selection jury **is** chaired by London's Roy Miles.

If the jury is being thought of as a group of separate individuals, then the plural is used:

The jury **are** about to hear it from the witness.

It is important to be consistent. So the example above should not be continued as follows:

The selection jury is chaired by London's Roy Miles. **They include** several famous people. ✗

It should be:

The selection jury is chaired by London's Roy Miles. **It includes** several famous people. ✓

colon

A punctuation mark with three main uses:

■ to introduce a list:

There are two other varieties of cedarwood oil: Texas (*Juniperus ashei*) and Virginian (*Juniperus virginiana*).

■ to introduce a piece of direct speech, or a quotation:

At once he said: 'I do not mean your immediate brief journey.'

■ to separate two parts of a sentence where the first leads on to the second:

And that is the end of the poor man's hopes: there is no return to eligibility.

See also: **commas, colons, and semicolons**.

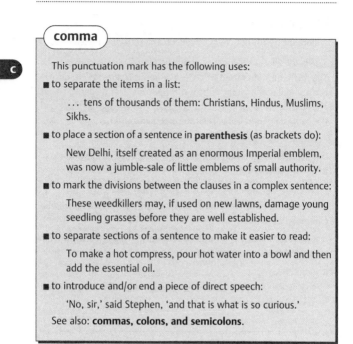

comma

This punctuation mark has the following uses:

■ to separate the items in a list:

> ... tens of thousands of them: Christians, Hindus, Muslims, Sikhs.

■ to place a section of a sentence in **parenthesis** (as brackets do):

> New Delhi, itself created as an enormous Imperial emblem, was now a jumble-sale of little emblems of small authority.

■ to mark the divisions between the clauses in a complex sentence:

> These weedkillers may, if used on new lawns, damage young seedling grasses before they are well established.

■ to separate sections of a sentence to make it easier to read:

> To make a hot compress, pour hot water into a bowl and then add the essential oil.

■ to introduce and/or end a piece of direct speech:

> 'No, sir,' said Stephen, 'and that is what is so curious.'

See also: **commas, colons, and semicolons**.

commas, colons, and semicolons

These three punctuation marks are all used to mark off different sections within a sentence. It is sometimes difficult to decide which to use. The decision is sometimes a matter of personal style, but the guidelines that follow will help in a large number of cases. The separate entries for the three punctuation marks contain additional information.

■ When introducing a piece of direct speech a comma is used much more frequently than a colon. A colon can be used for special effect:

> Intrigue is our mother's milk. We say: 'He is an excellent fellow, but ... '

A colon is also used to introduce an extended quotation.

■ Commas are normally used between the items in a list, unless each item is quite extensive. If so, a semicolon is used:

> Weeds may reach the lawn in various ways: as seeds blown by the wind; carried by birds; brought in on muddy footwear, machinery, or tools; or concealed in unsterilized soil or badly made compost used for top-dressing.

■ A semicolon marks a much stronger division within a sentence than a comma. It can be used to separate two sections which might otherwise form separate sentences.

> The essential oil found in jasmine flowers is too delicate to be produced by distillation; the heat tends to destroy the odour.

In the sentence above, the semicolon could be replaced by a full stop, but this would separate two ideas that are closely related. As it stands the sentence has a clear balance, with separate but linked ideas pivoting on the semicolon. It is wrong to use a comma to link sections of a sentence in this way.

■ If the first part of a sentence introduces an idea which appears in the second part, then a colon is better than a semicolon:

> Many consumers are against it: about three out of ten say it's never a good thing, and most others see it as an occasional necessity rather than as having positive advantages.

common noun

Nouns can be divided into two groups: common nouns and proper nouns. **Proper nouns** are those that refer to people, places, and things that are unique, for example *Manchester* and *William Shakespeare*. All nouns that are not proper nouns are grouped together as common nouns.

comparative

The form of an **adjective** that is used when comparing things. For example:

> He is **taller** than me.

The comparative is formed in different ways according to the length of the base adjective:

■ If it has one **syllable**, then the letters *-er* are added: *great → greater*.

■ If the word has three syllables or more then the word *more* is added before the adjective: *more attractive*.

■ Words of two syllables vary: some add *-er* and some use *more*. Some even do both, for example *clever → cleverer/more clever*.

The use of *more* and the adding of *-er* should not be combined, so it is wrong to say, for example, *more better*. ✗

complement

A **clause** component that completes an earlier part. Clauses can have a **subject complement**:

It	is	a shy forest animal.
subject	**verb**	**subject complement**

or an **object complement**:

It	made	him	angry and irritable.
subject	**verb**	**object**	**object complement**

complex sentence

A sentence with a main clause and at least one subordinate clause introduced by a subordinating conjunction. Examples of complex sentences are:

She told him	that	she did not play again for over a week.
main clause	**subordinating conjunction**	**subordinate clause**

If	it rains	everything in the shed will get wet.
subordinating conjunction	**main clause**	**subordinate clause**

When	the children came back from school	they found	that	still nothing had changed.
subordinating conjunction	**subordinate clause**	**main clause**	**subordinating conjunction**	**sub-ordinate clause**

compound sentence

A sentence with two or more main clauses joined by a coordinating conjunction. Examples of compound sentences are:

Then he came in,	and	she sat down quickly.
main clause	**coordinating conjunction**	**main clause**

Either	you agree with it	or	you don't agree with it.
coordinating conjunction	**main clause**	**coordinating conjunction**	**main clause**

compound word

A word composed of two other words. Examples include:

crime reporter   air-conditioned   scarecrow

As the examples show, the two words that form the compound are sometimes written separately, sometimes linked by a hyphen, and sometimes joined together. For many compounds there is a standard way, but other compounds can be written in more than one way. For example:

paper knife   paper-knife   paperknife

concession

To concede something is to admit its truth, usually after you have originally denied it or refused to admit that it may be true. An **adverbial** or **adverbial clause** of concession is one that says in effect, 'Yes, even though A was true, B happened.'

Adverbial clauses of concession

There are three main types:

■ Beginning with the **conjunction** *although*:

Although she always wanted to be a writer, **subordinate clause**	the theatre has claimed a lot of her energy. **main clause**

The writer finds the information contained in the main clause (that she has worked a lot in the theatre) is surprising in the light of the subordinate clause (that she wanted to be a writer).

■ In another type of concession clause the information contained in the subordinate clause may well be true, but it doesn't affect the truth of the information in the main clause:

Even if she took it into her head to come back early, **subordinate clause**	she wouldn't be back till half four at the earliest. **main clause**

■ In a third type the main clause contains information that is true, despite the truth of the information in the subordinate clause:

Tom supplements their pension by working part-time, **main clause**	even though he is nearly 70. **subordinate clause**

The main conjunctions used to introduce adverbial clauses of concession are:

although	despite	even if	even though
except that	not that	though	whereas
while	whilst		

It is also possible to have **non-finite clauses** of concession. For example:

> **In spite of being so fair**, his skin had taken on quite a deep tan in the few days they had been there.

There are also verbless clauses of concession:

> **Although a competent fighter**, Stretch was not considered to be one of the game's bigger punchers.

Adverbials of concession

Sentences may also contain phrases which express similar ideas to clauses of concession.

> It had been a happy marriage, **in spite of the difference in their ages**.

> This works **even with the quickest and most agile spiders**.

concord

Another word for **agreement**.

concrete noun

A **noun** which refers to something that can be seen, touched, heard, tasted, and/or smelled. Concrete nouns are contrasted with **abstract nouns**.

condition

When writing or speaking, we often wish to show that one event depends on another in some way. This is frequently done using an **adverbial clause** of condition:

> **If the weather was fine**, Maud liked to walk in Hyde Park.

One statement, *Maud liked to walk in Hyde Park*, is conditional upon the other: *the weather was fine*.

Conditional clauses are usually introduced by either *if* or *unless*. They can express a number of different meanings.

Common events

They can state general truths, such as:

> **If water penetrates window sills, doors, or their frames**, the result is wet rot.

In sentences like this the verb is in the **present tense**. It is also possible to used the **past tense** to describe general truths about the past:

If the tide was coming in, his ships had to stay tied up.

Possible events

Conditional clauses can describe situations which have not yet happened, but are possible:

If it comes to court you two can testify.

Here both verbs are in the present tense. Similar sentences can be constructed using *unless*:

Policemen don't find bodies **unless they are sent to look for them** ...

Here *unless* has the meaning of *if ... not ...* :

Policemen don't find bodies **if they aren't sent to look for them** ...

Future events

Very often conditional clauses speculate about events in the future. Such clauses can be open or closed. In an open conditional the speaker expresses no opinion about whether the future event is likely to happen or not. The verb in the *if* clause is in the present tense, and the verb in the main clause usually begins with *will*:

If they succeed in that, Germany's economy and its workers will be better off.

(The writer has no opinion of whether they will succeed or not.)

In a closed condition the writer makes it clear that the future event is more or less unlikely. In this case the verb in the *if* clause is in the past tense, and the verb in the main clause usually begins with *would*:

If I had time then I would say yes, but as it is, school work is taking priority.

Past events

Conditional clauses can also be used to speculate about how things might have turned out in the past:

If they had been her own children, she would have used them differently.

(But they weren't her own children, so she treated them as she did.) The condition cannot be fulfilled because it is impossible.

Clauses that are not introduced by a conjunction

It is possible to construct conditional clauses that do not begin with *if* or *unless*. The commonest way of doing this is to begin the clause with one of these words:

were   should   had

For example:

Were I to own a new BMW car, another ten microcomputers would be at my command, so their advertisements claim.

Should you succeed in becoming a planner, you would be helping to create these parameters.

Had I ignored my fitness, I could never have played international cricket for 20 years.

conjunct

A type of **adverbial** used to show the connection between a sentence and an earlier sentence. They are used in a variety of ways, including:

Adding and listing

In narratives, explanations, and arguments we often want to place items in a particular order. We indicate this fact and show the order by using words like *firstly*:

Firstly, the feeling for the tradition is very strong in the village; **secondly**, Gawthorpe is an ancient settlement—its history can be traced back to a Viking chief named Gorky and there is evidence that it existed in Roman times; **thirdly**, the original custom was to bring in a new May tree each year.

Sometimes the sequence is less important, but we still wish to make it clear that items are linked, by using words such as *furthermore*:

In addition to normal problems, such as security, food, and rest, the battalion had to contend with the fact that we would lose vehicles to mechanical failure, while only having two designated recovery assets. **Furthermore**, once everything was off the boats and we transformed into our tactical load plans, it became clear the battalion wanted to move a lot more equipment than originally planned.

Sentence adverbials used in this way also include:

also	as well	at the same time	besides
finally	first	in addition	last
meanwhile	moreover	next	soon
then	too		

Giving examples

Sometimes we wish to introduce an example or list of material which exemplifies part of the argument:

These birds are not evenly distributed along the coast. **For example**, scoter are mainly confined to East Sussex and mergansers to West Sussex ...

Other words used in this way are:

namely   as follows

Saying things another way

We may also wish to restate something using different words:

Oil also became the main source of funds for investment in industry, agriculture, health and education, and the nation's infrastructure. Oil revenue enabled the state to break its financial dependence on its citizens. **In other words** the state no longer needed its citizens to collect taxes to finance its activities.

Cause and result

In texts that contain an argument one sentence is often the logical development of what has gone before:

The nation's filmmakers, like its people, can't express emotion; they lack drive and passion, they're tame and repressed. **As a result**, the British can write novels and plays, even produce an occasional world-class painter but, when it comes to cinema, they might as well forget it.

Other sentence adverbials of this type are:

| accordingly | as a result | consequently | hence |
| so | | therefore | thus |

Contrasts and alternatives

A sentence can be contrasted with what has gone before:

The speed of sound in water is roughly four times as great as it is in air. **On the other hand**, water is not much different for taste and smell, and much worse for vision.

Other sentence adverbials of this type are:

all the same	alternatively	anyway	by contrast
conversely	even so	however	instead
nevertheless	on the other hand	rather	yet

Concession

Another type of contrast is similar to that used in adverbial clauses of concession: despite this fact, the following is true. For example:

On each occasion, the TAYAD supporters, who had done nothing else but peacefully distribute legal leaflets, narrowly escaped being lynched after police intervened. **Nevertheless**, the police detained the victims for provoking the public.

Other sentence adverbials of this type are:

even so   however   yet

See also: **paragraph**.

conjunction

A class of words that are used to join together words, phrases, or clauses. They fall into two groups.

■ **coordinating conjunctions**

These link items that have equal status grammatically:

uncomfortable **but** safe

ice cream **or** frozen yoghurt

Henna arrived **and** they called room service.

The commonest coordinating conjunctions are *and, or, but*.

■ **subordinating conjunctions**

If the two items being linked do not have equal status, then a subordinating conjunction is used. Most commonly this happens in complex sentences when a main clause is joined to a subordinate clause:

Businesses fail	because	they can't pay their bills.
main clause	**subordinating conjunction**	**subordinate clause**

Further information

The information given above is summed up in the diagram below, which also contains individual conjunctions. Each of the words in bold type has its own entry, where further information can be found.

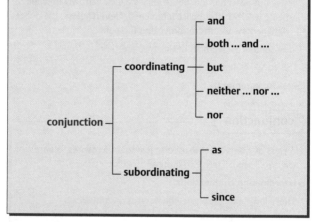

conjunction
- coordinating
  - and
  - both ... and ...
  - but
  - neither ... nor ...
  - nor
- subordinating
  - as
  - since

connective

This is not, strictly speaking, a grammatical term. It is used when describing how a text is linked together and can refer to:

■ an **adverbial** (an **adjunct** or **conjunct**)

■ a **conjunction** (**coordinating** or **subordinating**).

consonant

Writing

There are 21 consonant letters:

b c d f g h j k l m n p q r s t v w x y z

Speech

In speech a consonant is a sound that is made by blocking the flow of air while speaking. For example, the first sound in the word *mark* is made by closing the lips briefly, while the last sound is made by pressing the blade of the tongue up against the hard palate. There are 22 consonants in spoken English. They are the first sounds in each of the following words:

bat	char	cut	dip	fat	gut	hot
jar	late	meet	neat	pat	rate	ship
sip	that	thing	tip	vat	zip	

plus the sounds in the following words marked by letters in bold type:

mea**s**ure   si**ng**

Two other sounds are sometimes called consonants and sometimes semivowels. They are the first sounds in these words:

win   young

content word

Words can be divided into content words like *tree* and structure words such as *because*. Content words 'contain' meaning, and if you look them up in a dictionary you will find a definition of that meaning. The four classes of content words, **adjectives**, **adverbs**, **nouns**, and **verbs**, are also referred to as 'open' classes, since new words continue to be added to them as the language develops.

continuous aspect

The verb **aspect** which communicates the idea that an action continues over a period of time. It can be:

■ **present tense**

> Couples need to feel they **are building** something together that has meaning.

■ **past tense**

> Someone tried to set fire to the mansion they **were building** in River Oaks.

■ **future tense**

> When they run out of inventory, they **will be building** at a much lower level.

conversion

The process by which a **word** from one **word class** is used as if it belonged to another class. For example, *glue* started life as a **noun**, but is now frequently used as a **verb**. Many conversions are so common that we no longer notice them, but conversion is also a feature of creative uses of language:

> 'I really have some severe doubts regarding this partnership,' said he, **upping** and **awaying**.

It can also, however, lead to cliché and jargon:

> The current erratic supply of diesel has **impacted** negatively on the business community ...

coordinating conjunction

A **conjunction** that joins two items of the same grammatical status. The commonest coordinating conjunctions are:

> and   but   or

They can be used to link:

■ **words**

> biscuits **or** chocolate

■ **phrases**

> sports shops **and** large department stores

■ **clauses**

> I am working part-time, **but** my maternity leave begins next month.

could

A **modal auxiliary verb**, the past form of *can*. It can refer to ability in sentences that are about the past:

> She **could** not move.

It can also refer to possibility in the future:

> Mind you, I s'pose I **could** always return as a newt ...

With *have* it can refer to possible past events:

> She **could** not have failed to hear them.

countable and uncountable nouns

There are certain words which can only be used with **countable nouns** and not with **uncountables**. Other words can only be used with uncountables and not with countables.

WORDS	COUNTABLE	UNCOUNTABLE	EXAMPLE
little, less, least	✗	✓	little sustenance
few, fewer	✓	✗	few children
much	✗	✓	much food
many, several	✓	✗	many surprises

countable noun

A **noun** that has both a singular and a plural form. Most nouns are countable, because they refer to things that can be counted. A small number of nouns do not regularly have a plural form and are called **uncountable**.

dare

A **verb** that can be used as a normal verb and also as a **modal auxiliary verb**. For this reason it is sometimes described as a 'semi-modal verb'.

As a normal verb it is followed by the **infinitive** form of the verb:

> He **dared** to criticize the leader outright.

As a modal auxiliary verb it is followed by the verb **stem**:

But I **dare** say you like apples.

It can also stand alone in expressions such as:

Don't you **dare**!

---

dash

A punctuation mark that looks like an extended **hyphen**. It comes in two sizes: an em dash (—) and an en dash (-).

Em dash
An em dash is used to mark a break in sentences:

■ It can be used in pairs to show words in **parenthesis**:

In brute material terms he was an accomplice—in fact, a conspirator—to the murder of millions of children.

■ It can introduce something that develops, or is an example of, what has gone before:

You must have seen it, I'm sure—the blue flag with a white square in the middle.

In more formal writing a colon would be used instead of a dash.

■ It can introduce an aside by the writer:

I occupied Piers' old studio and Toby the three guest rooms—this purely for company.

■ In direct speech it can show that someone breaks off in mid sentence, or is interrupted:

I smiled and she said, 'You mean you want me to—'

Traditionally there is no space before or after an em dash. In modern typography, the em dash is increasingly being replaced by an en dash with a space before and after it:

In brute material terms he was an accomplice - in fact, a conspirator - to the murder of millions of children.

En dash
An en dash is used to show sequences:

1999-2000
an A-Z guide

> When it is used in this way there is no space before or after it.
> When describing sequences, either use *from 1999 to 2000* or
> *1999–2000*; mixing the two styles (e.g. *from 1999–2000* ✗) is
> wrong.

declarative

A form of clause or sentence used to make statements. In a
declarative the normal word order is for the **subject** to precede the
verb:

SUBJECT	VERB	REST OF SENTENCE
Happiness	is	no laughing matter.
Someone	might have warned	the poor girl.

defining relative clause

Relative clauses add information to the noun or pronoun they
modify. Sometimes that information is essential; without it the
sentence doesn't make much sense:

WITH RELATIVE CLAUSE	WITHOUT RELATIVE CLAUSE
A person **who is mentally handicapped** is just as much a member of society as anyone else.	A person is just as much a member of society as anyone else.

Removing the relative clause *who is mentally handicapped* makes a
nonsense of the sentence, because we do not know which person is
being described. Essential relative clauses of this type are called
defining relative clauses.

See also: **non-defining relative clauses, relative clauses and
punctuation**.

demonstrative pronoun

The demonstrative **pronouns** are:

     this   that   these   those

They are pronouns when they stand alone. When they are used before a noun, they are referred to as demonstrative **determiners**.

> In the beginning, **this** was all pretty intimidating. (pronoun)

> The waste steppes of southern Poland and Russia are covered with **this** plant. (determiner)

When referring to physical items, *this* and *these* can be used to indicate things that are nearer to the speaker by contrast with *that* and *those* which indicate things that are further away. Often, however, demonstrative pronouns are used more metaphorically. *That* or *those* is frequently used to distinguish the thing referred to from something that has gone before:

> ... in fact, glass soft-drink bottles cost about 5.5p, while **those** made from plastic are around half a penny more ...

This and *these* on the other hand are used to tie a statement in to something that has gone before:

> ... there were just six new diagnoses of MRSA bloodstream infection over the last year in Harrogate. At least half of **these** were cases in which patients brought MRSA into the hospital with them ...

derivational morphology

The study of how words are derived from other words. For example, the word *fortune* can form the basis of a number of words derived from it: *misfortune, fortunate, fortunately, unfortunate*, and so on. The new words are formed by adding a **prefix** or a **suffix**, or both, to the original word.

determiner

A class of words that form an important part of many **noun phrases**. The determiner comes before the **noun** and helps to define it. Common determiners are:

a	an	the	
this	that	these	those
some	any	no	

▶

my	our	your	his	her	its	their
many	few	little	much			
other	last	next				
one	two	three	etc.			
first	second	third	etc.			
all	both					
half	third	etc.				

Further information

The following entries also contain information about determiners:
**article; each; fewer/less; possessive determiners and
pronouns.**

dialect

A version of a language spoken in a particular geographical area
or by a particular group of people. The English spoken in
Newcastle is different from that spoken by natives of north
Cornwall. Not only do speakers in these two areas have a
different **accent**, they also use a number of different words.
Different dialects may also use slightly different grammar. For
example, in Devon some people say 'They do have …' in
preference to 'They have …'. Such regional expressions are not
'wrong', they simply differ from **standard English**. They are
sometimes described as 'non-standard'.

digraph

Two letters written together to represent a single sound. For
example, these are consonant digraphs:

ch   ck   gh   ph   sh   th

There are also many vowel digraphs in English. For example:

ai   au   ea   ei   oa   oi   ou

For historical reasons, the letters 'a' and 'e' are frequently joined in
the older spelling of words such as *medieval*:

mediæval

The use of this digraph is, however, dying out.

diminutive

- A version of a noun that refers to a small version of something. Such diminutives are formed by adding a prefix:

   minibus

   or a suffix:

   notelet   kitchenette   duckling

- A version of a noun that indicates familiarity or fondness, formed by adding a suffix:

   Aussie   sweetie   footer   champers

- A short form of a personal name:

   Timothy → Tim   Katherine → Kath/Kate/Katy

diphthong

An element of **pronunciation**. A diphthong is a **vowel** sound that is composed of a sequence of two vowels. The vowel in the word *so*, for example, begins with the 'o' sound of *hot* and then glides into the 'u' sound of *put*. Other diphthongs are the vowel sounds in the following words:

   high   late   toil

Diphthongs should not be confused with **digraphs**.

direct speech

In stories, reports, and certain other types of writing, the words spoken by people can be reported (in **reported speech**) or quoted directly (direct speech). Direct speech uses a set of punctuation conventions to separate the words actually spoken from the rest of the text, so that the reader is not confused. The need for these 'rules' can be seen when we remove the punctuation from a piece of direct speech:

   He's very clever, you know. Very said Mr Datchery without enthusiasm. I mean, he's got a terrific lot of degrees and he's lived in all sorts of countries. So I guessed. There was a pause; then: but you didn't think he was clever, did you?

It is very difficult to follow what is going on. Here is the same text with the direct speech correctly punctuated:

'He's very clever, you know.'

'Very,' said Mr Datchery without enthusiasm.

'I mean, he's got a terrific lot of degrees and he's lived in all sorts of countries.'

'So I guessed.'

There was a pause; then: 'But you didn't think he was clever, did you?'

Standard rules

■ The words spoken are enclosed between inverted commas:

'He's very clever, you know.'

or

"He's very clever, you know."

■ If you normally use single inverted commas, then use double inverted commas for 'quotes within quotes':

Then she said, 'I did it because Henry said, "I don't care what you do".'

and vice versa:

Then she said, "I did it because Henry said, 'I don't care what you do'."

■ Every time there is a new speaker, start a new paragraph:

'He's very clever, you know.'

'Very,' said Mr Datchery without enthusiasm.

■ Each new piece of speech begins with a capital letter, even if it is not at the beginning of the sentence:

There was a pause; then: 'But you didn't think he was clever, did you?'

■ Each piece of speech should be preceded by a comma or colon:

There was a pause; then: 'But you didn't think he was clever, did you?'

- There should normally be a comma, full stop, question mark, or exclamation mark at the end of a piece of speech. This is placed before the closing inverted comma(s):

  'He's very clever, you know.'

  'Very,' said Mr Datchery without enthusiasm.

- If the piece of speech is interrupted or the speaker trails off, then it can be ended with a dash or three dots:

  'I shall, thank you. Is there anything—'

  'Anything new? No, nothing.'

disjunct

A sentence **adverbial** that provides some comment by the speaker or writer on the content of the sentence in which it appears. Disjuncts often come at or near the beginning of the sentence. In the sentences that follow, the disjuncts are printed in bold:

Admittedly, the enemy on this occasion was not Napoleon.

Fortunately, this year's monsoon was short but sharp, and improved water management has produced good floods.

They have, **wisely**, no intention of getting married for years to come.

Common disjuncts include:

actually	admittedly	basically
briefly	clearly	frankly
in general	obviously	perhaps
personally	possibly	presumably
remarkably	roughly	(un)fortunately

ditransitive verb

A **transitive verb** is a **verb** that is followed by an **object**, for example:

It	destroyed	the Highland way of life.
	verb	**object**

do

Some transitive verbs can be followed by two objects: a direct object and an **indirect object**.

We	gave	them	an early Christmas present.
She	told	me	the story.
subject	**verb**	**indirect object**	**direct object**

Verbs like this are described as ditransitive. They include verbs that refer to transferring something from one agent to another, such as:

give   hand   inform   pass   tell

do

A **primary auxiliary verb**. Like *be* and *have*, *do* can be used both as an auxiliary and as a **main verb**. It is a common and useful main verb in sentences such as:

They are **doing** a play.

Overcoats will **do** more than keep you warm this winter.

Another assassin is waiting to **do** him in.

As an auxiliary verb it is used:

■ to make negative statements:

Water lilies **do** not grow well if water is falling onto their leaves.

■ to form questions:

'**Do** you understand me?' he asked a second time.

■ to form **tag questions**:

Well, it doesn't matter about anyone else, **does** it?

They didn't act like police, **did** they?

■ for emphasis:

And he **does** like to travel.

■ to avoid repetition:

I think you all know him better than I **do**.

This is instead of:

I think you all know him better than I **know him**.

dummy subject

In most sentences the subject indicates what the sentence will be about:

Many people in the industry see illegal file sharing as theft.

Some sentences, however, begin with a subject that contains no such information:

It was bright and sunny.

There is absolutely nothing there.

It and *there* are called dummy subjects: they do not provide information; they simply serve to start the sentence off. (To see how useful they are, try expressing the same information in a different way.)

each

A word that can be used in two ways:

■ **pronoun**

There were eight courses and it seemed that **each** lasted an hour.

... **each** of the 46 member countries of the Council of Europe ...

■ **determiner**

But prizes are also given to runners-up in **each** category.

Singular or plural?

Most of the time, *each* is singular and should be followed by a singular verb:

For although their personal relationship came to an end in the 1980s, and **each has** since remarried ...

... **each song is** intricately linked to the next ...

It is true that, in theory, **each of these acts is** a crime for which the police could prosecute.

The exception to this is when *each* comes immediately after a plural pronoun or noun to which it refers. Then the verb should be in the plural:

Taking their test results, **they each begin** looking at them.

The girls each prepare for the adventure.

either ... or ...

A pair of **coordinating conjunctions** that are used to link items that have the same grammatical status:

> ... the couple's three children **either** have degrees **or** are working on them.

It is easy to place one of the two in the wrong place. For example:

> ... either because a person looked stupid, or was made to look stupid by another person ... ✗

Here the two ideas being linked are:

> a person looked stupid

> a person was made to look stupid

Since *a person* appears in both, it is better to place *either* after it:

> ... because a person **either** looked stupid, **or** was made to look stupid by another person ... ✓

See also: **neither ... nor ...**; **or**.

either/or question

A question in which the speaker offers a choice of two possible answers:

> Is email a letter or a conversation?

Here the possible answers are 'a letter' or 'a conversation'. However, the respondent can always dodge the issue with a reply such as:

> I don't know; a bit of both, really.

Either/or questions, along with **yes/no questions**, are sometimes referred to as 'closed' questions, because they restrict the possible answers that can be given. This is by contrast with **wh- questions**, which allow a wide range of answers, and are 'open' questions.

ellipsis

The omission of one or more words in order to avoid repetition. It is often done by replacing a complete verb phrase by an auxiliary verb. Other clause components can also be omitted. Ellipsis is frequently used:

■ with contrasting subjects, objects, or adverbials:

> **You've** got more use for it than **I have**.

instead of

> You've got more use for it than I have use for it.

- with the verbs *be* and *have*:

> I was sure it would be worth the effort of breaking them in—and it **was**.

instead of

> I was sure it would be worth the effort of breaking them in—and it was worth the effort of breaking them in.

- with modal auxiliary verbs like *should* or *could*:

> Two of them disappeared without trace as fast as they **could**.

instead of

> Two of them disappeared without trace as fast as they could disappear without trace.

Ellipsis helps to give a text **cohesion**, by indicating to the reader or listener that sentences and parts of sentences are linked.

embedded clause

A **clause** which forms part of another clause, or of a **phrase**.

Within a clause

A **noun clause** can form the subject, object, or complement of a complex sentence. When this happens, it is embedded within the clause structure of that sentence. For example:

subject	verb	complement
This	is	**what they want to do.**

Within a phrase

Normally grammar follows the pattern that words form phrases, which combine to form clauses. Clauses can then stand on their own as **simple sentences**, or combine to form **compound** and **complex sentences**. So the hierarchy is: word—phrase—clause—sentence.

The exception to this pattern is when a **relative clause** forms part of a **noun phrase**:

a quirky story about a girl	who defies all odds to live her dream
	embedded relative clause
noun phrase	

etymology

e

The study of the history of words, or the history of a particular word.
Dictionaries often provide information about the etymology of
words. For example, from the *Oxford Dictionary of English*:

ramekin

> *noun* a small dish for baking and serving an individual portion of
food

- **origin** mid 17th cent.: from French *ramequin*, of Low German or
Dutch origin; compare with obsolete Flemish *rameken* 'toasted
bread'.

exclamation mark

The main use of the exclamation mark is to end sentences that
express:

■ an exclamation

'With a fixed bayonet! A fixed bayonet!' he repeated
incredulously.

■ direct speech spoken loudly or shouted

'The first one ... the first!' everybody yelled.

■ something that the writer or speaker finds amusing

Her son was the biggest poacher—he was a devil: he'd rob
your house in the middle of the day and let you see him!

It can also be used in brackets after a statement that the writer
finds amusing or ironic:

I look ruddy, muscly, well covered (!) and just, shall we say,
solid.

exclamative

An exclamation is a remark expressing surprise, delight, pain, anger, or other strong emotion, often spoken with extra force or emphasis:

How wonderful!

In writing, exclamations are often shown by the use of an exclamation mark.

Sentences of this kind can have a special grammatical construction: the exclamative. This involves changing the normal sentence order and starting the sentence in one of two ways:

■ the sentence begins with *how* + adjective

How strange it looked from below!

(instead of *It looked strange from below*.)

■ the sentence begins with *what* + noun phrase

What an incredible confidence trick the election polls have turned out to be.

(instead of *The election polls have turned out to be an incredible confidence trick*.)

In speech particularly, exclamations frequently contain no verb:

How stupid of me!

fewer/less

In formal writing and speech, *fewer* should be used with **countable nouns** and *less* with **uncountable nouns**. Examples:

Fewer shades of green

Parliament would have **less** power.

It is not standard English to use *less* with a plural or a number higher than one, as in the following example:

Less people vote in Euro elections than vote in local elections. ✗

finite verb

A form of the verb that is complete in itself and can be used alone as the **verb phrase** in a sentence. In the sentences that follow there is one finite verb which is printed in bold type:

Then I **examined** the three main rooms.

Science **tells** us about the structural and relational properties of objects.

The finite form of the verb shows **tense** (in the strict sense of present or past), **number**, and **person**.

The sentences that follow do not contain finite verbs; the verbs in bold type are non-finite:

Habit of **appearing to stand** on tiptoe, **stretching** the neck.

So kitsch, **frozen** in time.

If the verb phrase in a sentence consists of more than one verb word, then the first verb should be finite. In the sentences that follow, the verb phrase is printed in italics and the finite verb is in bold:

Magazine editors in 1955 *were hit* by the same problem.

The jazz scene *must have sounded* to Parker like a musical hall of mirrors.

A convenient way of checking whether a verb phrase is finite is to use the following flow chart:

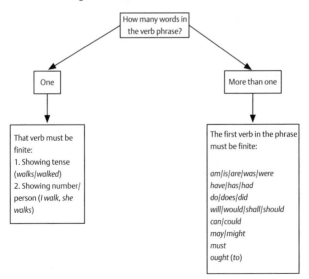

How many words in the verb phrase?

One

More than one

That verb must be finite:
1. Showing tense (*walks*/*walked*)
2. Showing number/person (*I walk, she walks*)

The first verb in the phrase must be finite:

am/*is*/*are*/*was*/*were*
have/*has*/*had*
do/*does*/*did*
will/*would*/*shall*/*should*
can/*could*
may/*might*
must
ought (*to*)

first person

The **personal pronouns** *I* and *we* are referred to as first person **singular** and first person **plural** respectively. When a story or report is written using the pronoun *I* it is said to be written in the first person, or to be a first person narrative:

I then went off for lunch, which was soup and crayfish.

focus

Some **adverbials** are used to focus attention on one part of a sentence:

Paul regularly runs out of the nursery to play ball in a busy street; he has **also** run home by himself and was nearly hit by a lorry.

The writer is adding to the dangerous things that Paul has done, and the adverb also helps focus our attention. If we remove the word, the sentence is much weaker:

Paul regularly runs out of the nursery to play ball in a busy street; he has run home by himself and was nearly hit by a lorry.

Other examples of sentences with focusing adverbials are:

Utah, **in particular**, needs all the new employers it can find.

Only the flowers in the vase on the table in front of me seemed real.

fraction

See **numeral**.

full stop

Full stops are used:
- to mark the end of a sentence:

    And then you put it in the mail, and you repeat this process ad infinitum until the damn thing sells.

- to mark the end of a group of words that is not a full sentence, but which is complete in itself:

    Over and over. Again and again. Relentlessly.

- after abbreviations that consist of the first part of a word:

  Sept.   Thurs.

- in email and website addresses:

  www.oup.com

future continuous

A **tense** formed by *will be* or *shall be* followed by the **present participle**:

I shall be working.

Uses

- To describe a future action, but emphasizing that it will go on over a period of time:

  I **shall be working** quite late tonight.

- To refer to planned or arranged events in the future:

  Mr Wilkins **will be working** at the library during the next year.

- To make promises or threats:

  I **will be making** an announcement to the audience before the curtain rises.

future perfect

A **tense** formed by *will have* or *shall have* followed by the **past participle**:

She **will have worked**.

Uses

- To predict that a future action will be finished by a particular time:

  When I retire later this year at 56 I **will have completed** 38 years with the company.

- To make deductions:

  Jennifer **will have had** enough by now.

  We're sure club members **will have worked** very hard to make this event a great success.

future perfect continuous

The **tense** used to describe an action that will have been completed at a particular point in the future. It emphasizes that the action will have been going on over a period of time. It is formed by *shall/will have been* followed by the **present participle**:

Some readers **will have been growing** roses for years.

future tense

This is also called the simple future **tense**. It is formed by using the **modal auxiliary verbs** *will* or *shall* followed by the verb **stem**:

you **will tell**

For example:

You **will tell** me, eventually.

Uses

■ Prediction:

You **will arrive** in your resort mid-morning on 12 May.

■ Indicating determination or commitment:

The Labour Government **will** immediately **make** available £1bn to invest in the NHS.

■ To show ability (in general terms, not just in the future):

A pair of kitchen scales **will do** that easily.

■ To describe habits:

Feminists **will keep** on about language.

gerund

See **verbal noun**.

grading adjectives

Modifying an **adjective** by placing one or more **adverbs** in front of it. For example:

a beautiful view

a **rather** beautiful tropical garden

extremely beautiful drawings

Only **qualitative adjectives** can be graded. **Classifying adjectives** cannot normally be graded.

grammar

Grammar is a word with a variety of meanings. In this book it is used to refer to the rules by which words are changed and ordered to form sentences. The study of how words change is called **morphology**; the description of how words are organized into phrases, clauses, and sentences is called **syntax**.

Grammar can be descriptive or prescriptive. Descriptive grammar seeks to describe how language is used in the real world, in all its variety. Prescriptive grammar sets out rules which should be followed if you wish to speak or write 'correct' or 'good' English. Sometimes these 'rules' are based on proper observation of the way in which educated speakers actually use the language. At other times they are based on prejudice, or on what the speaker was taught at school, often many years ago.

Further information

A selection of words relating to the study of grammar is shown in the diagram below. Each of the words in bold type has its own entry, where further information can be found.

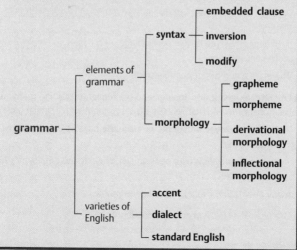

g

grapheme

A term from linguistics meaning the smallest unit in writing that can change meaning. This is a letter or group of letters representing a single **phoneme**, for example:

b   ng   ea.

head/headword

The head or headword of a **phrase** is the word on which the phrase is built up:

	HEADWORD	EXAMPLE
noun phrase	**noun**	a large **jug** of water
verb phrase	**verb**	have been **seeing**
prepositional phrase	**preposition**	**by** the roadside
adjective phrase	**adjective**	very **big** indeed
adverb phrase	**adverb**	rather too **slowly**

he, she, or it?

In English there isn't a pronoun that can refer to a person without defining whether that person is male or female. This raises the problem of how to avoid choosing between *he* and *she* in sentences like this:

If your employee is over pension age, —?— pays no employee's NI contributions.

There are a number of possible solutions:

■ Use *he* throughout and apologize to the reader, explaining that you mean *he* or *she*. Alternatively use *she* throughout with a similar gloss.

If your employee is over pension age, **he** pays no employee's NI contributions.

If your employee is over pension age, **she** pays no employee's NI contributions.

Many people find this approach unacceptable.

■ Use *he or she* (and *him or her*) throughout:

If your employee is over pension age, **he or she** pays no employee's NI contributions.

This is generally acceptable but can be rather longwinded and clumsy, especially if used a lot.

■ Turn the sentence into the plural:

If your employees are over pension age, **they** pay no employee's NI contributions.

This is both acceptable and neat, but sometimes it is not possible.

■ Use the pronouns *they/them*, even though the noun they refer to is singular:

If your employee is over pension age, **they** pay no employee's NI contributions.

This is increasingly used, but traditionalists disapprove because they consider it ungrammatical. For this reason it should be avoided in more formal writing.

■ Turn the sentence into the passive:

No employee's NI contributions need be paid by employees over pension age.

This is often a neat solution, provided that the sentence isn't too long and doesn't become difficult to understand.

homograph

Two words which are written in the same way but which have different meanings and are pronounced differently are described as homographs. An example is *sow*, which can mean to put seeds in the ground, but when pronounced differently refers to a female pig.

See also: **homonym**.

homonym

Two (or more) words which look or sound the same, but have distinct and unrelated meanings. These fall into three groups:

■ Words which are written and pronounced in the same way:

    seal   butt   last   mew

■ Words which are written in the same way but pronounced differently:

   sow   lead

These are also referred to as **homographs**.

■ Words which sound the same but are written differently:

   meet/meat   right/write/rite

These are also referred to as **homophones**.

homophone

See **homonym**.

how

An **adverb** with four main uses:

■ to introduce a **question**

   How are you feeling?

■ to introduce a **noun clause**

   This is **how** they did it.

■ with an **adjective** or another adverb

   You have no idea **how** heavy flowers can be.

   He had noticed before **how** slowly the British matured.

■ to introduce an **exclamative**

   How remarkable!

In informal usage it can also be used as a **noun**:

   To the buyer, the **how** has become as important as the what.

however

An **adverb** with two main uses:

■ to modify an **adjective** or another adverb:

   We cannot afford to postpone necessary actions, **however**
   difficult, in the future.

■ as a sentence **adverbial**, a **conjunct**:

> There was, **however**, one important difference.

This is the traditional way to use the word, enclosed between commas. It can also be placed at the beginning of the sentence, followed by a comma:

> **However**, they may not need a bus much longer.

hyphen

A punctuation mark with three uses:

Spelling
Some **compound words** are linked by a hyphen. There is no simple rule to help know which compounds need hyphens and which do not. Hyphens are, however, being used less and less, especially in compound nouns. People tend to write *website* rather than *web-site* and *air raid* rather than *air-raid*.

Hyphens are still often used in the following situations:

■ to form a verb from a compound noun:

> a booby trap → to booby-trap
>
> The area was heavily mined and **booby-trapped**.

■ to form a noun from a **phrasal verb** or a **prepositional verb**:

> to build up → a build-up
>
> The **build-up** to a major event is really exciting ...

■ (sometimes) to form a word with a prefix:

> co-opt   multi-storey

■ to form certain compound adjectives:

> easy-care   right-handed

Sentence construction (syntax)
Sometimes it is important to show that certain words in a sentence are meant to be read together. If the hyphen(s) were not used, the meaning might not be clear. Compare these two sentences:

I wonder if he's thought of a **ready-to-wear** collection.

I felt newly sophisticated and was **ready to wear** black with aplomb!

Typesetting

Hyphens are also used in printed texts to split words that will not fit onto the end of a line. There are rules about how words should be split, which can be found in some dictionaries. Many computer word-processing and desktop publishing programs offer a choice between automatic and manual hyphenation.

if

A **subordinating conjunction** used to introduce conditional clauses (see **condition**).

It can also be used:

■ with *what* to form questions about things that might happen in the future or might have happened in the past:

What if I find certain issues or situations difficult?

What if he had become much more ruthless in that time?

■ before an adjective or adverb to form a **verbless clause**:

It was a delicious, **if small**, compensation.

Trade unions began, **if slowly and unadventurously**, to assert that they didn't give a hoot.

I/me

I is the **subjective** form and *me* is the **objective** form of the **first person** pronoun.

■ The subjective form should be used for the **subject** of a sentence:

My husband and **I** own six dogs.

In formal language it should also be used for the **subject complement**:

It is **I** who am wrong, not you.

Increasingly in less formal language *me* is used in such sentences:

> Come on, this is **me**, remember?

■ The objective form should be used for the object of a sentence:

> For all I know you've manipulated both William Ash and **me** into this whole situation!

It is also used after a preposition:

> Which is how it was **with** my husband and **me**.

■ In some **dialects** *me* is used as the subject of the verb:

> 'Cos **me** and him are good friends, like.

This is not **standard English** and some speakers work so hard to avoid it that they use *I* when they should use *me*. For example:

> This is just another publishing trick to make you and **I** talk about it—which we are. ✗

In this sentence the pronoun is the object of the verb *make* and so it should be *me*:

> This is just another publishing trick to make you and **me** talk about it—which we are. ✓

The commonest example of this misuse of *I* is expressions using *between*:

> The most important thing between you and **I** is our mutual love, is it not? ✗

As *between* is a preposition, this should be:

> The most important thing between you and **me** is our mutual love, is it not? ✓

imperative

The imperative **mood** is used to make commands:

> 'Go away!' cried Mary.

The **verb** form used is the **stem**. Imperative **clauses** have a special form. They resemble a normal clause, but there is no **subject**. In effect the subject is *you*, but is not stated:

> '(You) go away!' cried Mary.

indefinite pronoun

The indefinite **pronouns** are:

some	someone	somebody	something
any	anyone	anybody	anything
none	no one	nobody	nothing
everyone	everybody	everything	all
either	neither	both	each

As the name 'indefinite' suggests, these allow the speaker to be rather vague about who or what is referred to:

> I do believe that **somebody** must find a way to wrestle control of the Internet from the hands of the US and the corporate interests and give it back to the people of the world.

indirect object

Certain **transitive verbs** can have two **objects**:

■ a direct object

■ an **indirect object**.

For example:

We	gave	them	an early Christmas present.
She	told	me	the story.
subject	**verb**	**indirect object**	**direct object**

As the examples show, the two types of object convey a different meaning. The indirect object tells us about the person or thing that benefits from the action described by the verb: *they* received the early Christmas present; *I* heard the story.

Verbs which commonly have an indirect object as well as a direct one include:

bring	buy	give	promise
send	show	teach	tell

infinitive

A form of the **verb**. In the **verb phrase** the infinitive has two forms:

- the verb **stem**. This form of the infinitive is used after **modal auxiliary verbs** such as *must* and *should*:

Life	must		go	on.
	modal auxiliary		**infinitive**	

- *to* plus the verb stem:

I	want	to save	her.
	verb	**infinitive**	

infinitive clause

A **clause** in which the verb is not **finite**, but an **infinitive**. The following examples show the similarities and differences between the two types of clause:

CLAUSE TYPE	FINITE CLAUSE	INFINITIVE CLAUSE
noun	I want **what is best for my little girl**.	All I really want is **to have a home of my own**.
relative	And that was another thing **that was troubling her**.	There was only one thing **to do** in these circumstances.
adverbial	Physiotherapy is important **so that hands, arms, legs, etc. are kept mobile**.	Robert made sure his head was back far enough, **so as to avoid the swinging chain**.

inflection

Most **nouns** and **verbs**, many **adjectives**, and some **pronouns** change their form according to how they are used in a sentence. This process is called inflection.

■ Nouns inflect to show the **plural**:

 one car → several cars

 one child → several children

■ Verbs inflect to show **number** and **person** in the present tense:

 I work → she works

They also inflect to show the difference between **past** and **present tenses**:

 I work → I worked

 I write → I wrote

There are also inflections to form the **present participle**:

 write → writing

and the **past participle**:

 write → written

■ Some adjectives inflect to make the **comparative** and **superlative** forms:

 tall → taller → tallest

■ Some pronouns inflect to form the **objective case**:

 she → her

and the **possessive case**:

 her → hers

inflectional morphology

The study of the way in which the form of words is changed according to the way in which they are used in sentences.
See **inflection**.

intensifier

An **adverb** that is used to **modify** an **adjective**. Intensifiers show how much of a quality something has. For example:

 a beautiful view

 a **rather** beautiful tropical garden

 extremely beautiful drawings

Intensifiers can also modify other adverbs. For example:

> easily
>
> **fairly** easily
>
> **incredibly** easily

interrogative

The type of **sentence** or **clause** used to ask questions. There are four main types of question:

- **either/or questions**
- **tag questions**
- **wh- questions**
- **yes/no questions**.

interrogative pronoun

The interrogative pronouns are:

> who   whom   whose   what   which

They are used in the formation of questions:

> So **what** do we, the taxpayers, get for $880 million?
>
> 'So,' said Jenco, '**whose** are they?'

intonation

An element of **pronunciation**. Intonation refers to the musical 'tune' of a sentence. It is possible to speak the following words in two ways:

> So she went home after that

- as a statement:

> So she went home after that.

In this case the voice rises slightly towards the end of the sentence, but falls at the very end.

- as a question:

> So she went home after that?

Here the voice rises at the end of the sentence, making it clear that it is a question and not a statement.

Intonation is used in many different ways to put a 'spin' on a spoken sentence. For example, the following sentence can be spoken in two different ways:

So she went home after that, didn't she?

- with the voice falling at the end. This indicates that the speaker is expecting listeners to agree.
- with the voice rising at the end. In this case the speaker expresses uncertainty and is looking for either confirmation or correction:

A: So she went home after that, didn't she?

B: No, she stayed on for another couple of hours.

intransitive verb

A **verb** that does not have to be followed by an **object**. For example:

groan: The man on the terrace was groaning.

laugh: We both laughed.

Verbs that are followed by an object are referred to as **transitive**. Some verbs can be either transitive or intransitive. For example, *write*:

Why hadn't Ken told him he was writing?

She was writing an essay.

inversion

Changing the normal order of elements in a sentence. For example, some questions are formed by reversing the normal order of **subject** before **verb**:

She is breathing. → Is she breathing?

This reversal of subject and verb is sometimes used in **direct speech**, too:

'It looks like you sure got a lot,' **said she**.

inverted commas

Punctuation marks used to separate a group of words from the rest of the text. They can be single:

   'and'

or double:

   "and"

They are used as follows:

Direct speech

   'He's very clever, you know.'

   'Very,' said Mr Datchery without enthusiasm.

See also: **direct speech**.

Titles

In handwritten documents and in some printed texts, inverted
commas are used for the titles of books, pictures, plays, films, and
TV programmes:

   'The Taming of the Shrew'

   'On the Waterfront'

In print, titles are more commonly shown by the use of italics.

Quotations

When a text includes a direct quotation from another book, or from
what someone has said, quotation marks are used to mark it off:

   Alan Lomax calls the work song a 'spiritual speed-up'.

But if the passage to be quoted is fairly long it is often set out
differently on the page, usually by indenting:

   The African musicologist Nicholas Ballanta-Taylor describes it:

      Music in Africa is not cultivated for its own sake. It is
      always used in connection with dances or to
      accompany workmen. The rhythmic interest of the
      songs impels them to work and takes away the
      feeling of drudgery ...

When this is done, inverted commas are not necessary.

'Not my idea'

A similar use is when writers want to make it clear that an
expression is not their own, or one that they would choose:

   Many larger houses were being split up into so-called
   'flats'.

In this example the use of *so-called* signals the writer's feeling, but the inverted commas will do the job on their own:

Many larger houses were being split up into 'flats'.

Single or double

There is no fixed rule about whether to use single or double inverted commas, but the following guidelines may help.

■ Choose either single or double as your default style and use them consistently. Single inverted commas tend to be preferred in Britain and double in the US.

■ If you need to include a quotation within a quotation, enclose it in the type of inverted commas you have not yet used. So if you normally use single inverted commas, put the enclosed quotation in double:

'He wondered if that was what was before them, but did not say anything. Best not to know. "The story has to be finished, and I must be the one to finish it." The words were like stones in his mouth.'

and vice versa:

"He wondered if that was what was before them, but did not say anything. Best not to know. 'The story has to be finished, and I must be the one to finish it.' The words were like stones in his mouth."

irregular verb

A verb that does not form its **past tense** and **past participle** in a regular way. Regular verbs work like this:

STEM	PAST TENSE	PAST PARTICIPLE
happen	happened	happened
tango	tangoed	tangoed
smile	smiled	smiled

If the stem ends in a consonant or a vowel other than *e*, then you add the letters *ed*. If the stem ends in *e* then the letter *d* is added.

Irregular verbs do not follow this pattern. Linguists divide them into seven different groups within which there are patterns. For everyday purposes it is simpler to divide them into three:

■ verbs in which the stem, the past tense, and the past participle each have a different form

■ verbs in which the past tense and the past participle have the same form which is different from the stem

■ verbs where all three are the same.

GROUP	STEM	PAST TENSE	PAST PARTICIPLE
1	take	took	taken
	swim	swam	swum
2	swing	swung	swung
	bind	bound	bound
3	hit	hit	hit
	burst	burst	burst

There are two verbs which are even more irregular: *be* and *go*.

STEM	PRESENT TENSE	PAST TENSE	PAST PARTICIPLE
be	is/am/are	was/were	been
go	go/goes	went	gone

is/are

Verbs have different forms in the simple **present tense** depending on the **number** and **person** of the subject. For the verb *to be* these are:

	SINGULAR	PLURAL
1st person	I am	we are
2nd person	you are (thou art)	you are
3rd person	he/she/it is	they are

It also has different forms in the simple **past tense**:

	SINGULAR	PLURAL
1st person	I was	we were
2nd person	you were (thou wert)	you were
3rd person	he/she/it was	they were

It is important to make sure that **subject** and **verb** agree, and if the subject is a single **noun** or a short **noun phrase** there isn't usually a problem. In longer sentences, especially where the subject is an extended noun phrase, difficulties can sometimes arise. For example:

> One very key official has told the Prime Minister that the machinery, funding, and general ability to mobilize a strong but swift campaign **is** in place. ✗

The subject of the clause is *the machinery, funding, and general ability to mobilize a strong but swift campaign*. This is formed of three noun phrases joined by *and*:

the machinery	funding	**and**	general ability to mobilize a strong but swift campaign

So it must be plural not singular and the verb should be *are*.

In the sentence that follows the error has a different cause:

> Israel's five hours of talks with Syria, which started on Sunday after much diplomatic wrangling, **was** described as frustrating. ✗

Here the writer has made the verb agree with the noun phrase that is nearest to it: *much diplomatic wrangling*. In fact the subject is:

> Israel's five hours of talks with Syria, which started on Sunday after much diplomatic wrangling ...

To be sure of the correct form of the verb it is necessary to identify the **headword** of the noun phrase—the word that lies at its heart. What was the writer talking about when he said that it was 'frustrating'? The answer has to be 'five hours'. And as *hours* is plural, the verb must be plural too.

it + passive

In formal writing it is quite common to begin a sentence with *it* followed by the passive form of the verb. For example:

It is felt that a person propelling a motorcycle with his legs astride the cycle and his feet on the ground by 'paddling' it would be driving.

The sentence is taken from a legal text, so it needs to be precise. 'It is felt' is imprecise because it is unclear who it refers to. (And *felt* is rather a vague term.) Better to say:

If someone sits astride a motorcycle and uses their feet to 'paddle' it along the ground, then, in law, they are driving.

See also: **passive voice**.

its/it's

This is an occasion where the use of the **apostrophe** can cause problems. The rule is as follows:

its

This is the possessive form (see **case**; **possession**):

His face had lost **its** boyish roundness.

it's

This is the short form of *it is* or *it has*:

It's a sign of growing up.

just

This **adverb** has two meanings:

■ a short time ago:

He and his wife have **just** arrived here.

■ only:

I **just** had time to see my mother and sister off.

Sometimes it is not clear which of the two meanings is intended:

I've **just** bought this little flask.

Does this mean that the speaker only bought the flask and nothing else? Or that the speaker has bought it very recently? If you wish to be absolutely precise you may have to replace *just*, and/or add other words:

I've **only** bought this little flask—**nothing else**.

I bought this little flask **just now**.

lexical morphology

The study of how new words are formed by adding **prefixes** or **suffixes** to existing words. For example:

un + attractive + ness → unattractiveness

lexical pattern

Another term for **word family**.

lexical verb

Another term for **main verb**.

lexis

The words that are used in a language, or a **dialect** of a language. More specifically, 'lexis' refers to the words which carry meaning, in contrast with those that are used to 'glue' a sentence together, and form part of grammar. So, for example, *people*, *purple*, and *perplex* are lexical items; *in*, *might*, and *someone* are grammatical items.

Although 'vocabulary' is a more commonly used noun with much the same meaning, it does not have a related adjective as lexis does: *lexical*.

See also: **lexical morphology**; **lexical pattern**; **lexical verb**.

like/as/as if

Like is used as a **preposition** to show similarity between things:

Was it that he looked so much **like** his father?

In informal speech and writing it is also used as a **conjunction** in sentences such as:

He looks **like** he's never seen an iron.

Purists frown on this use of *like* and consider it 'uneducated' even though this usage dates back at least as far as Shakespeare. (Darwin, for example, wrote, 'Unfortunately few have observed like you have done.') If you wish to avoid this kind of criticism, in formal writing and speech, use *as* or *as if*:

He looks **as if** he's never seen an iron.

Unfortunately few have observed **as** you have done.

linking verb

Main verbs can be divided into:

■ **transitive**

■ **intransitive**

■ **linking**.

Linking verbs are used to link the **subject** of a **clause** with its **complement**. They are used in sentences like these:

subject	linking verb	complement
All the rumours	were	true.
That	seems	healthy.

By far the commonest linking verb is *be*. Others are:

    seem   appear   become   look

lists

It is quite common to have to include lists of items in a piece of continuous prose. Punctuation has two purposes in presenting such lists:

1. To introduce the list

If the list itself is not particularly long, there is no need to use any punctuation to introduce it:

    He had come equipped with a bottle of white wine, pâté, French bread, and fruit.

Longer lists, especially in formal writing, can be introduced by a **colon**:

    Weeds may reach the lawn in various ways: as seeds blown by the wind ...

This can also be done less formally by a **dash**:

It contained quite a bit of information—the position of the police telephones, the infirmaries, the hospitals, fire brigade, fire boxes, and so on.

2. To separate the items in the list

This is normally done by placing a **comma** after each item:

He had come equipped with a bottle of white wine, pâté, French bread, and fruit.

If each item in the list is quite long, **semicolons** are sometimes used instead of commas:

Weeds may reach the lawn in various ways: as seeds blown by the wind; carried by birds; brought in on muddy footwear, machinery, or tools; or concealed in unsterilized soil or badly made compost used for top-dressing.

Comma before 'and'?

The last item in a list is usually preceded by *and*. Some writers and publishers always place a comma before this *and*:

In fact, English criminal law has a wide range of such offences, of which those involving firearms, offensive weapons, motor vehicles, and other endangerment will be outlined here.

Other writers do not. This is partly a question of individual style. But the comma before *and* is sometimes necessary. Two items joined by *and* can appear to belong together. If you read the sentence that follows without much care it may seem rather strange:

Other sources of calcium, if milk does not agree with you, are yoghurt, cheese, shrimps and ice cream.

'Shrimps and ice cream'? A comma would avoid any such momentary confusion:

Other sources of calcium, if milk does not agree with you, are yoghurt, cheese, shrimps, and ice cream.

main clause

Every full sentence contains at least one main **clause**. Sometimes two (or more) main clauses are linked together using coordinating conjunctions to form a compound sentence:

main clause	coordinating conjunction	main clause
Aja knew everyone in town.		
No man can face this situation without uneasiness	and	these circumstances were exceptional.

The two clauses in the last example can be joined in other ways, by making one of them dependent on the other: by turning it into a **subordinate clause**.

main clause	subordinating conjunction	subordinate clause
No man can face this situation without uneasiness	so	these circumstances were exceptional.

subordinating conjunction	subordinate clause	main clause
Although	no man can face this situation without uneasiness	these circumstances were exceptional.

main verb

The **verb phrase** in a **clause** can contain two types of **verb**: main verbs and **auxiliary verbs**. Main verbs carry a meaning that can be looked up in a dictionary. (They are also referred to as 'lexical verbs'.) If the verb phrase only contains a single verb, then that must be a main verb. If it contains more than one, then one will be a main verb and the other(s) auxiliary. In the examples that follow, the main verb is in bold type and the auxiliary verb(s) in italics.

Strange men **moved** about the streets in pairs.

Everything now *was* always **reminding** me of something else.

In the end my legs *seem to have* **got** better on their own.

manner

Adverbials and **adverbial clauses** can be used to provide information about how things occur.

■ Adverbials

She drifted **slowly** over to the telephone.

The trees rushed past **at great speed**.

■ Adverbial clauses

> She had arrived early, **as she always does**.

> Ted was a child of the sixties, but he sounded **as if he'd been born in the Blitz**.

It is also possible to have **non-finite clauses** of manner:

> He made **as if to get ready to leave**.

may

A **modal auxiliary verb** with two types of meaning:

■ permission

> Thank you, Mrs Prynn, you **may** leave us now.

■ possibility

> They **may** come in handy.

See also: **can/may**; **may/might**.

may/might

These two **modal auxiliary verbs** can be used to talk about possibility in the present, future, or past.

Present and future

Either *may* or *might* can be used:

> They **may** come in handy.

> You **might** want to add to a set of chairs that you already possess.

Past

There are three types of past situation in which *may* or *might* can be used.

■ The speaker does not know whether something happened or not and is just speculating about it. Here we can use *may* or *might*:

> Suspicions remain that MacKenzie was linked to organized crime in some way, but officers believe he **may** have made a serious mistake over a single loan around 1999.

> He **might** have thought about his wife, his daughter, or even about his mother.

■ The speaker knows that an event did not happen and is speculating about how things might have turned out if circumstances had been different. In this case, you should only use *might*:

If the grandmother hadn't spoiled the boy so badly, Jin **might** have had a better future. ✓

It would be wrong to write:

If the grandmother hadn't spoiled the boy so badly, Jin may have had a better future. ✗

■ In a report, the event being described is completed and the possibilities referred to have also been closed down. Here only *might* can be used:

He had no doubt that they were dealing with a suicide bomber and that he **might** have to shoot him dead. ✓

The following would be wrong:

He had no doubt that they were dealing with a suicide bomber and that he **may** have to shoot him dead. ✗

The use of *may* continues the possibility into the present, when it is clear that the situation is in fact over and done with.

might

A **modal auxiliary verb** used to indicate possibility.
See **may/might**.

modal auxiliary verb

An auxiliary verb that forms part of a verb phrase which refers to events that are potential rather than actual:

Almost all of them **have achieved** personal bests. (actual)

If he had not played football, who knows what he **might have achieved** as a scientist, philosopher, or politician? (potential)

The modal auxiliary verbs are:

shall	**will**	**should**	**would**
can	**could**		
may	**might**		
must			
ought (to)			

Each of these has a separate entry in this book.

Dare and **need** can also be used as modal auxiliaries:

> The Cathedral authorities did not **dare** call the police again.

> Not that they **need** know that yet, of course.

These, too, have separate entries.

Modal auxiliaries can convey a wide range of different meanings: see **modal meanings** for more about this.

modal meanings

Modal auxiliary verbs can be used to convey a wide range of meanings. The table below illustrates some of the commonest, but it is by no means exhaustive.

MEANING	VERBS USED	EXAMPLE
Ability	can, could	I need interpreters in my surgery who **can** speak Punjabi, Urdu, and Gujarati.
Potential	can, could, might, ought to, should, will, would	A suitable satellite in high orbit **should** do it nicely.
Permission	can, could, may, might	Candidates **may** enter for both examinations, if desired.
Requests and invitations	can, could, may, might, will, would	**Will** you come with me?
Offers, promises, threats	can, could, shall, should	The Company **will** keep a copy of all material delivered to the Publisher.
Prediction	could, may, might, should, will	It **could** be dangerous for anybody who knows.
Obligation	must, ought to, should	Every volunteer **must** do at least one shift on the phones every fortnight.

| Advice | could, might, must, ought to, should | 'Perhaps you **could** try waders,' suggested Preston. |
| Habitual actions | might, will, would | Every afternoon she **would** wake from her afternoon sleep and cry pitifully, sometimes for as long as two hours. |

modify/modifier

In **grammar**, to modify is to change or add to the meaning of a word or phrase. A modifier is a word or group of words that changes or adds to the meaning of another word. For example:

■ **Adjectives** modify **nouns**.

■ Nouns can also be modified by other nouns and by **prepositional phrases**.

In the examples that follow, the modifiers are printed in bold.

Edgar Degas favoured his studio to the **open** (adjective) air, preferring to paint at the racecourse and in **ballet** (noun) studios.

There was a smear **of mud** (prepositional phrase) on his nose.

■ **Adverbs** modify **adjectives**.

Isabella can **very** (adverb) easily come across as a prig.

Modifiers that come before the word they modify are referred to as **premodifiers**:

open air

Those that follow the word they modify are **postmodifiers**:

smear **of mud**

See also: **adjective phrase**; **adverb phrase**; **noun phrase**.

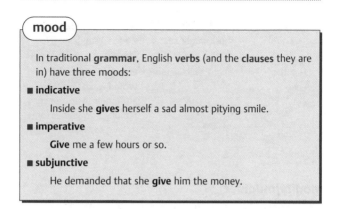

mood

In traditional **grammar**, English **verbs** (and the **clauses** they are in) have three moods:

■ **indicative**

Inside she **gives** herself a sad almost pitying smile.

■ **imperative**

Give me a few hours or so.

■ **subjunctive**

He demanded that she **give** him the money.

morpheme

The lowest unit of language that can convey meaning. You cannot break a morpheme down into anything smaller that has a meaning. Many simple words are morphemes. For example:

  child   shed   walk

Some words consist of two or more morphemes:

  child + ren   child + ish
  walk + s   walk + ing

ren, ish, s, ing all convey some meaning, even though none of them is a word in its own right. If we try to break them down any further we just end up with **graphemes** or **phonemes**:

  r + e + n   i + sh

None of these conveys meaning on its own.

morphology

The study of how words are built up and how they change according to their use in sentences. With **syntax** it forms the **grammar** of the language. This can be shown in the following sentence:

  Bharati's words gave him an idea.

Morphology tells us, for example, that the plural of the noun *word* is formed by adding the letter *s*, and that the verb *give* is **irregular** and its **past tense** is *gave*. Syntax tells us that the sentence is **simple** and is made up of a **subject**, **verb**, **indirect object**, and **direct object**.

multiple sentence

A **sentence** that contains more than one **finite clause**. (As opposed to a **simple sentence** that only contains one finite clause.) Multiple sentences are divided into **compound sentences** and **complex sentences**.

must

A **modal auxiliary verb** used to express a number of meanings, including the following:

■ likelihood/logic

    You **must** be starving.

■ compulsion/obligation

    In such cases there **must** be a right of appeal.

■ morality

    However, we **must** not hate them.

■ determination

    'I **must** go,' breathed Stefania, and was gone.

■ advice

    You really **must** get out of that bad habit.

See also: **modal meanings**.

need

A verb that can be used as a normal **main verb** or as a **modal auxiliary verb**. For this reason it is sometimes described as a 'semi-modal' verb.

■ As a main verb, it is a **transitive verb** (one that requires an object):

    They **needed** clothes that would not get torn in a fight.

m

n

■ As a modal auxiliary verb, it is followed by *to* and the **stem** of a main verb:

> They **needed to** rest, they said, but showed no signs of doing so.

In questions and negative statements the *to* is omitted:

> **Need** I say more?

> He **need** not have worried.

negative

English **clauses** can be positive or negative. The commonest way of making a negative clause is by adding *not*:

> I have made my mind up.　→　I have **not** made my mind up.

If the verb is in the simple **present** or the simple **past**, then it is necessary to add the auxiliary *do*:

> I **do not blame** her.

> The attainment of independence for India **did not mark** the end of its struggle.

Other entries on negatives are: **neither**; **neither . . . nor . . .**; **none are/none is**; **none/no one**.

neither

Neither can be used in three main ways:

■ as a **determiner**

> It's baffling that **neither** team has scored in this match yet.

Used in this way, the **noun phrase** containing *neither* is followed by a singular verb.

■ as a **pronoun**

> While both men have a long list of achievements to their credit, **neither** is in the first flush of youth.

> **Neither** of these skills is necessary any more.

Normally *neither* as a pronoun is followed by a singular verb, but sometimes writers use a plural verb after *neither of* to achieve an emphatic effect:

Neither of these candidates **have** accepted tainted money.

■ with *nor*: see below.

neither ... nor ...

Coordinating conjunctions that can be used to link words, phrases, and, sometimes, clauses:

The victor was **neither** Apple **nor** IBM.

A number of points should be remembered:

■ *Neither* is normally only used with two items, so it is non-standard to say:

Neither sound, nor earth, nor sky could be seen here.

(Even after allowing for the fact that sounds cannot be 'seen'.)

■ The two items to be joined must be grammatically equivalent, and it is important to get *neither* in the right place. Here it is not:

I **neither** cared about the characters nor their predicaments. ✗

This should be:

I cared about **neither** the characters nor their predicaments. ✓

n

nominal clause

Another name for a **noun clause**.

non-defining relative clause

Relative clauses add information to the **noun** or **pronoun** they **modify**. Sometimes that information is essential: without it the sentence doesn't make much sense. Other relative clauses are not essential to the sentence as a whole: they may add interesting information, but if they are removed the sentence still stands.

WITH RELATIVE CLAUSE	WITHOUT RELATIVE CLAUSE
The minister, **who had red hair and fire in his eye**, started on an upbeat note.	The minister started on an upbeat note.

The information contained in the relative clause *who had red hair and fire in his eye* is interesting, but even when it is removed we still know to whom the sentence refers. Clauses of this kind are called non-defining relative clauses.

See also: **defining relative clause**; **relative clauses and punctuation**.

none are/none is

People sometimes say that you should always follow the **pronoun** *none* with a singular verb. They argue that *none* is derived from *not one* so it must always be singular. This is mistaken. Both are acceptable in educated speech and writing. In speech, and with phrases containing *none of*, a plural verb is more frequently used than a singular one. In writing, the situation is reversed. Where *none* is used on its own, then a singular verb is more commonly used. The best advice is to follow *none* with the form of the verb that makes best sense in the context:

> Of the five bridges crossing the Tyne at Newcastle, **none is** more famous than the High Level Bridge.

> There do not appear to have been any children (**none are** mentioned in his will).

In the first sentence the writer implies that even if you examine the bridges **one by one**, you will not find one that is more famous. In the second sentence the writer is concerned with *children* and so it makes sense to use the plural form of the verb.

none/no one

The pronoun *none* can refer to one individual person or more than one (as explained in the previous entry). In contemporary English *no one* is more frequently used if you wish to refer to a single person. For example:

> University lecturers frequently complain about the standard of Leaving Cert students arriving in college these days, but I bet **none are** as dumb as the professor who was conned out of €15 500 by an internet scam.

> New music is the hardest to play because **no one is** really familiar with it ...

non-finite clause

A **clause** which is used in the same way as a finite clause, but does not have a **finite verb**. Instead it has an **infinitive**, a **present participle**, or a **past participle**. In the examples that follow, the non-finite clause is in bold type and is followed in brackets by a finite version of the same structure.

■ infinitive

You just don't know **when to stop**. (. . . when you should stop.)

■ present participle

Every person has a responsibility for maintaining safety **when travelling**. (. . . when they are travelling.)

■ past participle

They are cooled by water **taken from the River Yenisey**. (. . . that is taken from the River Yenisey.)

non-restrictive relative clause

Another name for a **non-defining relative clause**.

nor

A **coordinating conjunction**. It is often used as part of a pair: **neither . . . nor . . . .**

n

noun

Nouns are words used to refer to people, places, things, and ideas. As a grammatical class, nouns satisfy most or all of the following tests:

■ **number**: they have a singular and a plural form.

one car, two cars   one child, several children

■ **determiners**: they can be preceded by *a, an,* or *the.*

a child   an apple   the cars

■ **modifiers**: they can be modified by an adjective placed before them.

a young child   a ripe apple   the new cars

■ **phrases**: they can form the **headword** of a noun phrase.

> a ripe red apple ready to eat   the new cars on the forecourt

Further information

Nouns fall into a number of broad groups, each of which has a separate entry:

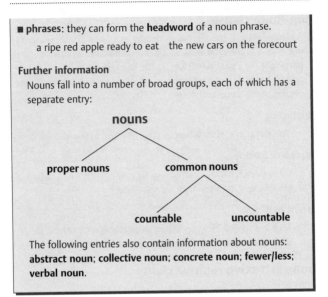

The following entries also contain information about nouns:
abstract noun; collective noun; concrete noun; fewer/less; verbal noun.

noun clause

A **clause** in a **complex sentence** forming one of the following elements:

■ **subject**

> **What they want to do next** is to use deuterium and tritium in the machine.

■ **object**

> We don't just let them do **what they want to do**.

■ **subject complement**

> This is **what they want to do**.

■ **object complement**

> He made it **what it is today**.

A noun clause can also be the object of a **preposition**:

> Women make their own minds up **about what they want to do**.

noun phrase

A group of words built up on a single **noun**, which is called the **headword** of the **phrase**. The noun phrases that follow all have the same headword, *books*:

books

some books

some books about photography

some excellent books about photography

some really excellent books about photography

Noun phrases can consist of the following parts:

DETERMINERS	PREMODIFIERS	HEADWORD	POSTMODIFIERS
some	really excellent	books	about photography
a		visit	to the Sierra Maestra
the two	frothy	cups	of cappuccino

In **clauses** noun phrases can be:

■ **subject**

   The only thing driving research into GM foods is greed!

■ **object**

   Harry lifted **his bushy eyebrows** at Elizabeth.

■ **subject complement**

   It was **a stirring tune**.

■ **object complement**

   But now the party faithful have appointed him **crisis manager of a party still threatened by disintegration**.

■ part of a larger phrase, for example a **prepositional phrase**:

number

crisis manager	of	a party still threatened by disintegration
		noun phrase

prepositional phrase

noun phrase

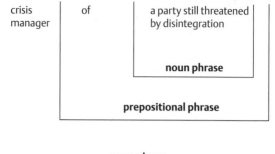

number

English grammar has two numbers, singular and plural. They are marked in the following ways:

Nouns

Most nouns have a singular and a plural form:

SINGULAR	PLURAL
house	houses
foot	feet

Pronouns

Many pronouns have a singular and a plural form. For example:

SINGULAR	PLURAL
I	we
he/she/it	they
this	these

Verbs

In the third person of the simple present tense verbs have a different form for singular and plural:

SINGULAR	PLURAL
she walks	they walk

See also: **agreement**.

numeral

There are three kinds of numeral: cardinal, ordinal, and fraction. Numerals can be used as **pronouns** or **determiners**.

Cardinal numerals

These provide information about quantity; they answer the question, 'How many?'

> The other **five** were federal judges ...

> You know we are given only **five** days to train with the foreign-based players ...

Ordinal numerals

These provide information about ranking position.

> It's on the **fifth** level, room 529.

> I'll be the **fifth**.

Fractions

These provide information about quantities less than one whole.

> According to Dr Piot, **two thirds** of young women in sub-Saharan Africa still do not know how HIV is transmitted.

> He is also entitled to a company car and **two thirds** salary as pension.

object

In a statement (**declarative**) **clause** the object normally comes after the **verb** and refers to a person, place, thing, or idea that is different from the **subject**. It can be a **noun**, a **pronoun**, a **noun phrase**, or a **noun clause**:

REST OF SENTENCE	OBJECT	TYPE
She lost	consciousness.	**noun**
She lost	it.	**pronoun**
She lost	her libel case.	**noun phrase**
Most families lost	what was virtually their only source of income.	**noun clause**

See also: **indirect object**.

object complement

Part of a **clause** that completes the meaning of the **object**. In statements it follows the object and refers to the same person, place, or thing:

subject	verb	object	object complement
She	appointed	him	deputy party chairman.

The object complement can be:

■ **noun**

> I appointed him **skipper**.

■ **adjective** or **adjective phrase**

> Cameron made him **uneasy**.

■ **noun phrase**

> Both the ancient universities made him **an honorary doctor**.

■ **noun clause**

> He made it **what it is today**.

objective case

See **case**.

omission marks

A number of dots, usually three, which are used to show that something has been missed out from a sentence. They have two main uses:

■ to reduce the length of a quotation, and/or to cut it down to its essentials:

> Endearing anecdotes about the great man follow, the sort that 'cling ... to all really great journalists'.

■ in **direct speech** to show that the speaker did not complete what he or she was saying:

> 'I really have to sit down.'

'Just see if you can go a little ...'

Zero collapsed.

Some writers prefer to use a **dash** for this purpose:

'I really have to sit down.'

'Just see if you can go a little—'

Zero collapsed.

only

A word that can be used as an **adjective**, an **adverb**, or a **conjunction**.

Adjective

As an adjective, *only* is normally preceded by *the* and followed by a noun or the **pronoun** *one*:

That will be the **only** way to keep the commercial sector healthy.

Bill was certainly not the **only** one nervous before the start of the big race.

Adverb

As an adverb, *only* is used to limit the meaning of the verb or another element of the sentence, or the whole sentence. It tells us that its application is restricted to that one item or event. The placing of *only* varies according to how it is used.

■ Applying to a **verb**

If the verb consists of just one word (the **main verb**), it comes immediately before it:

He **only** realized too late after things turned sour for him.

If the verb consists of more than one verb (**auxiliary verb**(s) followed by a main verb), *only* is placed after the first auxiliary verb:

The business could **only** survive through finding niches and performing well.

If the verb is *be*, then *only* follows it:

War is **only** a means of imposing a country's will over another by force for a while.

■ Applying to another **sentence** element

When *only* applies to other sentence elements it normally comes immediately before them:

It's shipping in 4 weeks, but initially **only** through the A&E website.

Conjunction

In less formal English, *only* is used as a conjunction with a similar meaning to *but*:

His features still had a handsome appearance, **only** he was now bearded and his hair was greyer.

Potential problems

Using *only* in the ways described above can sometimes lead to possible confusion, as in the following sentence:

He **only** touched the wrap with his fingers ...

This could mean that he touched the wrap but not the contents, or that he didn't touch the wrap with any other part of his body. In situations like this, if you wish to be absolutely clear you may have to move *only* so that is closer to the word(s) you wish to emphasize:

He touched **only** the wrap with his fingers ...

He touched the wrap **only** with his fingers ...

These versions may sound less natural, but they are more precise.

or

A **coordinating conjunction** used to link items of a similar grammatical status:

■ words

rain **or** shine, winter **or** spring ...

■ phrases

an operating system **or** a suite of office programs

■ clauses

They must still be at the market **or** they went to the bar for a drink.

Further information

See also: **either ... or ...**

ordinal

See **numeral**.

ought

A **modal auxiliary verb** used to refer to possible, rather than actual, events. It expresses a view about how desirable an action might be and is normally followed by *to* and the **stem** of the **main verb**:

You **ought to go** and see a doctor.

It can also stand alone:

No, I **ought** not.

Not used with 'did'

Ought is not used with *did* in **standard English**. So the following are both non-standard:

Did she **ought** to be there? ✗

The base didn't **ought** to be that close to local communities. ✗

These should be:

Ought she to be there? ✓

The base **ought** not to be that close to local communities. ✓

o

p

paragraph

Texts of any length written in continuous prose are usually divided into paragraphs. These are marked in print and writing by beginning a new line. There is usually also either a small gap between the paragraphs and/or the first line of a new paragraph is indented slightly.

Paragraphs are a useful way of helping the reader through a text. They are also useful to the writer in helping giving a text shape. Individual paragraphs usually have a typical pattern and are linked to each other in a variety of ways.

paragraph

Example

> Editing involves looking at the report and thinking about how it can be improved. Drafting, too, involves reading what you have written and thinking about how it can be improved. So what's the difference? It is a question of focus. When you draft you are thinking about yourself as writer: about what you want to communicate to your audience. When you edit, you think about your readers: you try to see things from their point of view.
>
> It is important to understand this distinction, because unless you do, you will find it hard to edit what you have written. In many ways the person who wrote a text is the worst person to be given the job of editing it. They have been working at it for hours, days—months, even—and find it difficult to stand back from it and look at it objectively and dispassionately. That is exactly what an editor has to do, but it is something that the author finds very difficult to achieve. (That's why, when I have finished writing this book, I shall hand it over—with some relief— to a professional editor, who will look at it with fresh eyes.)

Paragraph structure

A typical paragraph has three sections:

■ Lead sentence

(Sometimes called the topic sentence.) This is normally the first or second sentence in the paragraph and tells the reader what the paragraph is about:

> Editing involves looking at the report and thinking about how it can be improved.

■ Body of the paragraph

There follow a number of sentences, usually between two and five, that develop this subject matter. In this case there are four which examine the similarities and differences between editing and drafting.

■ Concluding sentence

This has two purposes: to round off and/or sum up what has gone before, and to provide a lead-in to the next paragraph.

In the case of the first paragraph in the example, the concluding sentence rounds off the 'argument' that editing is different from drafting:

> When you edit, you think about your readers: you try to see things from their point of view.

Links

If a text is to flow, the paragraphs need to be linked together. Here the second paragraph begins with the words:

> It is important to understand this distinction, because unless you do, you will find it hard to edit what you have written.

The words *this distinction* refer back to the content of the previous paragraph. The whole sentence explains how this paragraph will develop the ideas of the previous one.

See also: **ellipsis**; **reference**; **sentence adverbial**.

parenthesis

When something is put 'in parenthesis' it is separated off from the main part of the sentence, by a pair of brackets, commas, or dashes. This is usually because it contains information or ideas that are not essential to an understanding of the sentence. This may be because the words contain additional but non-essential information:

> Negotiation over issues deemed too controversial, such as the status of Jerusalem and the right of Palestinian refugees to return home (from exile in Lebanon, for example), were deferred to a future time.

or because they form a comment by the author on the rest of the sentence:

> This movie (by which I mean *Lord of the Rings* in total) will stand for generations as exemplar of film excellence ...

Brackets are the most formal (and most obvious) way of showing parentheses:

p

> Negotiation over issues deemed too controversial, such as the status of Jerusalem and the right of Palestinian refugees to return home (from exile in Lebanon, for example), were deferred to a future time.

Commas are less forceful:

> Negotiation over issues deemed too controversial, such as the status of Jerusalem and the right of Palestinian refugees to return home, from exile in Lebanon, for example, were deferred to a future time.

Dashes are the least formal:

> Negotiation over issues deemed too controversial, such as the status of Jerusalem and the right of Palestinian refugees to return home—from exile in Lebanon, for example—were deferred to a future time.

participle

A form of the **verb** that is used in forming **verb phrases** and for other purposes. There are two participles:

- **present participle**
- **past participle**.

The table below shows examples of these in **regular** and **irregular verbs**.

STEM	PRESENT PARTICIPLE	PAST PARTICIPLE
talk	talking	talked
swim	swimming	swum
hit	hitting	hit

As the table shows, in regular verbs like *talk*, the past participle is formed by adding *-ed* to the verb stem and has the same form as the past tense. In irregular verbs it is formed in a variety of ways, and may be different from the past tense (for example *swim/swam/swum*).

Participle problems

A present participle can be used to form a **non-finite clause**. If this is placed at the beginning of the sentence it should always refer to the **subject** of that sentence:

Travelling through time and space, the Doctor and Rose come face to face with a number of new and exciting monsters.

Here the present participle *travelling* is attached to the subject of the sentence, *the Doctor and Rose*.

Sometimes writers forget this and begin a sentence with a participle that is not attached to anything stated in the sentence. The participle is said to be 'hanging' or 'dangling'. For example:

Travelling to Finland, the weather got colder and colder. He wished he had brought more warm clothes with him. ✗

Grammatically this means that the weather was travelling to Finland, whereas what the writer means is:

As **he was travelling** to Finland, the weather got colder and colder … ✓

Good writing practice means avoiding 'hanging' or 'dangling' participles by making sure that the participle is attached to the subject of the sentence.

part of speech

See **word class**.

passive voice

Transitive verbs can be used in two different ways, called **voices**: active and passive.

Active: A warrior in a long cloak attacked them.

passive: They were attacked by a warrior in a long cloak.

In the passive voice it is as if the object of the sentence gets a voice of its own and can describe an event from its own point of view. This applies even if the original subject is inanimate:

active: A big wave hit the side of the paddle wheel …

passive: The side of the paddle wheel was hit by a big wave …

The transformation from active to passive works like this:

For example:

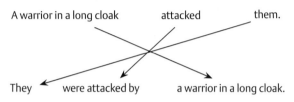

All the tenses that exist in the active voice can also occur in the passive, although some are rarely used:

	SIMPLE	CONTINUOUS	PERFECT	PERFECT CONTINUOUS
PAST	I was hit	I was being hit	I had been hit	I had been being hit
PRESENT	I am hit	I am being hit	I have been hit	I have been being hit
FUTURE	I shall be hit	I shall be being hit	I shall have been hit	I shall have been being hit

Passive or active?

Using the passive voice has a number of disadvantages:

1. It tends to sound rather formal and remote:

   Volunteers were sought to set up the tables.

2. It can lead to rather complicated expressions:

The opinions of staff and governors were sought and although there were some reservations it was decided that a questionnaire should be distributed to parents.

Sentence 1 would be better as:

They asked for volunteers to set up the tables.

Sentence 2 would be simpler if it were rewritten in the active voice:

We asked staff and governors for their views. Although not everyone agreed completely, we decided to send a questionnaire to parents.

On the other hand, the passive can make sentences shorter. For example, this:

She was run over by a car travelling at excessive speed and overtaking on the wrong side.

is better than:

A car travelling at excessive speed and overtaking on the wrong side ran her over.

The first sentence has a short subject *She* and is easy to follow. The subject of the second sentence is too long and we lose the sense before we get to the verb.

It + passive

Some writers like to begin a sentence with *It*, followed by the passive. For example, the following sentence concerns the options available to a woman who has been attacked:

It is considered that in the last resort it is to civil remedies that she should have recourse.

This is 'lawyer talk'. It is better to be direct and use the active voice:

We believe that in the last resort she will have to sue her attacker.

In some situations, however, the construction can be useful:

It is believed that similar reserves exist along the coast.

The writer may well not have a clear idea of exactly whose opinion is being quoted, although it is evident that the belief is widespread or well established.

See also: **active voice**; **voice**.

past continuous

This **tense** is formed by *was* or *were* followed by the **present participle** of the **main verb**:

he **was writing**

For example:
He **was writing** his speech at home.

Uses

■ To show how one event occurred during another event:

While they **were talking**, they heard a terrific roar.

■ To refer to a completed event that went on over a period of time:

I **was working** there in 1933.

past participle

One of the forms of the **verb**:

stem	smile
infinitive	to smile
present tense	smile/smiles
present participle	smiling
past tense	smiled
past participle	**smiled**

In **regular verbs** it is the same as the past tense form and is made by adding -*ed* to the verb **stem** (or just -*d* if the verb ends with the letter *e*). In **irregular verbs** it is formed in different ways.

The past participle is used to form a number of tenses:

■ **present perfect**: I have smiled

■ **past perfect**: I had smiled.

■ **future perfect**: I shall have smiled.

It is also used to form past tenses with **modal auxiliaries** (*I might have smiled*, *I should have smiled*, etc.).

past perfect

This **tense** is formed by *had* followed by the **past participle**:

she **had written**

p

Uses

■ To refer to an action in the past that continues up to, or relates to, a single point in the past:

> By 1428 they **had established** a city state.

■ To contrast two events, one of which happened before the other:

> I went round after I **had finished**.

■ To show a causal link between two events in the past:

> We swerved because someone **had run** a red light in front of us.

■ In narrative to give background information:

> It **had been** a bad year for Cliff.

past perfect continuous

This **tense** is formed by *had been* followed by the **present participle**:

> She **had been** writing

Uses

■ To refer to an action that continued over a period in the past:

> He **had been studying** hard for some hours.

■ In a report, to refer to a continuing action in the past contrasted with a single completed action in the past:

> In the two weeks that I **had been working** at the Addison Family Restaurant, I had managed to spill two bowls of steaming hot soup, nine ice cold drinks, and one salad on the customers, and was working up to the newest waitress nightmare award.

past tense

This is also called the simple past **tense**. It is used to refer to actions in the past. In **regular verbs** it is formed by adding *-ed* to the verb stem (or just *-d* if the verb stem ends in *e*):

> you **walked**

In **irregular verbs** there is a variety of past tense forms.

Uses

■ To refer to a single action in the past:

p

On 25 May 1812, the Felling pit in Durham **exploded**, killing 92 men and boys.

■ To refer to a regular or repeated action in the past:

They **met** several times last week.

The mobile shop **called** once a week.

perfect aspect

The verb **aspect** which communicates the idea that an action has been completed, but is relevant to another point either in the present or the past. It can be:

■ **present**

The target market for this well-known grocery store is an organic food shopper. However, not every item in the store is organic. Nor is every shopper seeking organic food. Yet they **have built** a countrywide chain by targeting a specific market.

The writer is concentrating on the present situation, and although the building of the chain of stores occurred in the past, it is still relevant now.

■ **past**

I got up, and headed for the fireplace they **had built** last night. There was still a spark of golden fire glowing in the wood ...

The fire was built the night before, but this is still of interest to the narrator at the moment s/he is describing.

■ **future**

I wonder what kind of lives they **will have built** for themselves when they turn 45 and can't really have any connection with people ...

The writer is looking into the future of these people—when they turn 45. By that time the 'life-building' will be complete, but it will be very relevant to them, aged 45.

person

Personal **pronouns** can be first, second, or third person, and **singular** or **plural**:

	SINGULAR	PLURAL
1st person	I	we
2nd person	you (thou)	you
3rd person	she, he, it	they

The person of the **subject** affects the form of the **verb** in the **present tense** (and in the **past tense** of the verb *to be*):

	SINGULAR	PLURAL
1st person	I work	we work
2nd person	you work (thou workest)	you work
3rd person	she, he, it works	they work

This applies even if the actual personal pronoun is not used. For example:

Mr and Mrs Hughes live ...

See also: **number**; **agreement**.

personal pronoun

A group of **pronouns** that refer to people, things, or ideas. They have three **cases**: **subjective**, **objective**, and **possessive**:

	SUBJECTIVE		OBJECTIVE		POSSESSIVE	
	SINGULAR	PLURAL	SINGULAR	PLURAL	SINGULAR	PLURAL
1st person	I	we	me	us	mine	ours
2nd person	you (thou)	you	you (thou)	you	yours (thine)	yours
3rd person	she, he, it	they	her, him, it	them	hers, his, its	theirs

p

phoneme

A distinctive speech sound. We express ourselves using words. In writing each word is made up of letters, and in speech a word is made up of a series of phonemes. There are 44 phonemes in

standard modern English, fairly evenly divided between
vowels and consonants. The phonemes in a word do not
correspond to the letters with which we write it. For example,
the word *singing* contains seven letters: *s-i-n-g-i-n-g*,
but only five sounds: *s-i-ng-i-ng*.

phrasal verb

A verb that consists of a **main verb** plus an **adverb**. Phrasal verbs
can be transitive or intransitive. For example:

INTRANSITIVE	TRANSITIVE
back away	carry out
catch on	dig up
hold on	leave behind
settle down	spell out

Transitive phrasal verbs

The adverb can come before or after the **object**:

> They've **dug up** a lot of human bones at my old uncle's house.

> They've **dug** a lot of human bones **up** at my old uncle's house.

But if the object is a **personal pronoun** the object normally comes
before the adverb:

> The wind **carried** it **out** over the reef and out to sea. ✓

not

> The wind **carried out** it over the reef and out to sea. ✗

If the object consists of a fairly long noun phrase, it is usually more
convenient to place it after the adverb—otherwise the reader is left
waiting for the completion of the verb. Compare these two versions
of the same sentence:

> Mr Lamont **spelled out** the tactics behind the battle for the
> pound.

> Mr Lamont **spelled** the tactics behind the battle for the pound
> **out**. (?)

See also: **prepositional verb**.

phrase

A group of words that forms part of a **clause**, or sometimes part of another phrase. A phrase is built up on a **headword**, and the types of phrase are named according to the class the headword belongs to:

	HEADWORD	EXAMPLE	USES IN A CLAUSE
noun phrase	noun	a large jug of water	subject, object, complement, or as part of a larger noun phrase
verb phrase	verb	have been seeing	verb
prepositional phrase	preposition	by the roadside	adverbial, or as part of a noun phrase
adjective phrase	adjective	very big indeed	complement, or as part of a noun phrase
adverb phrase	adverb	rather too slowly	adverbial

See also: **modify/modifier**; **postmodifier**; **premodifier**.

P

place

Adverbials and adverbial clauses can provide information about where something happened.

Adverbials

Adverbials of place can be individual words (**adverbs**) or **prepositional phrases**:

We should not have expected to see them **there**.

A quarter of them live **in New York City**.

Adverbial clauses

These are usually introduced by the conjunctions:

where   wherever   everywhere

For example:

Place them **where your customers can't avoid them**.

Wherever he went things seemed different.

Everywhere one looked there were unaccustomed trophies on display.

plural

See **number**.

---

possession

A term used in grammar to mean that something belongs to someone or something else.

With **nouns** we show possession by the use of the possessive **apostrophe**:

Sue's bungalow

the Government's admission

Pronouns change their form and can be used as **possessive pronouns** and **possessive determiners**:

SUBJECTIVE PRONOUN	POSSESSIVE PRONOUN	POSSESSIVE DETERMINER
I	mine	my
she	hers	her
you	yours	your

---

possessive apostrophe

The apostrophe can be used to show that something belongs to someone. For example:

the girl's handbag

the Browns' Silver Wedding anniversary

See **apostrophe** for the rules governing this.

possessive case

See **case**.

possessive determiners and pronouns

Personal **pronouns** have two **possessive** forms:

SUBJECTIVE FORM OF PRONOUN	POSSESSIVE PRONOUN	POSSESSIVE DETERMINER
I	mine	my
we	ours	our
she	hers	her
he	his	his
it	its	its
you	yours	your
they	theirs	their

■ Possessive pronouns are used on their own in a sentence:

   The manager has his problems but we have **ours** as well.

■ Possessive determiners always come before a noun:

   Fossils provide one of **our** most direct links with the prehistoric past.

postmodifier

A **modifier** that comes after the **headword** in a **noun phrase**, an **adjective phrase**, or an **adverb phrase**:

PREMODIFIER	HEADWORD	POSTMODIFIER
	property	**for sale in France**
rather	exceptional	**for a film of its age**
too	seriously	**by far**

predicate

That part of a **clause** which follows and completes the meaning of the **subject**. It always contains the **verb** and may also contain other elements (**object**, **complement**, **adverbial**).

SUBJECT	PREDICATE
The smile	vanished.
She	squeezed my hand.
The antique lamp above	bathed the room in a dim gold.

predicative use of adjectives

Adjectives can be used after a **linking verb** to form the **complement** of a **clause**:

SUBJECT	LINKING VERB	ADJECTIVE AS COMPLEMENT
Mechanical repairs	were	vital.
You	seem	sad.
Contracts	are becoming	anti-competitive.

This use is called predicative.

prefix

Part of a word that comes before the **base**. Prefixes add to or alter the meaning of the base word in some way, as can be seen by the following examples.

BASE WORD	PREFIX	PRODUCT
market	super-	supermarket
	hyper-	hypermarket
interested	un-	uninterested
	dis-	disinterested

Prefix meanings

PREFIX	MEANING	EXAMPLE
a-	not, not affected by	amoral
ante-	before	antecedent
anti-	against	anti-pollution
arch-	chief	archpriest

PREFIX	MEANING	EXAMPLE
auto-	self	autobiography
bi-	two	bipartisan
bio-	(from biology)	biodiversity
circum-	around	circumference
co-	joint, together	coordinate
contra-	opposite	contradiction
counter-	against	counteract
crypto-	hidden	crypto-fascist
de-	making the opposite of	demystify
demi-	half	demigod
di-	two	dialogue
dis-	making the opposite of	disagree
du-/duo-	two	duologue
eco-	(from ecology)	eco-tourism
Euro-	(from European)	Eurodollar
ex-	former	ex-husband
	out of	extract
fore-	in the front of, ahead of	forerunner
hyper-	very big	hypermarket
in-	not, opposite of	inexact
	in, into	insert
inter-	between	interstate
intra-	inside	intravenous
mal-	bad(ly)	maladministration
mega-	very large	megastar
mid-	middle	midlife
midi-	medium-sized	midi-length
mini-	small	minimarket
mis-	wrong, false	misadventure
mono-	one	monogamy
multi-	many	multi-layered
neo-	new	neolithic
non-	not, opposite of	non-partisan
out-	beyond	outreach
over-	too much	overreach

P

premodifier

PREFIX	MEANING	EXAMPLE
para-	ancillary	paramedic
	beyond	paranormal
poly-	many	polymath
post-	after	post-election
pre-	before	pre-election
pro-	for	pro-gun
	deputy	proconsul
pseudo-	false	pseudo-intellectual
re-	again	rerun
	back	reverse
retro-	backwards	retrograde
self-	self	self-sufficient
semi-	half	semi-serious
sub-	below	sub-zero
super-	more than, special	superhuman
supra-	above	suprasensuous
sur-	more than, beyond	surreal
tele-	at a distance	telematics
trans-	across	trans-Siberian
tri-	three	tripartite
ultra-	beyond	ultraviolet
	very much indeed	ultra-careful
un-	not, opposite of	unnecessary
under-	below, less than	underachieve
uni-	one	unitary
vice-	deputy	vice-chancellor

premodifier

A **modifier** that comes before the **headword** in a noun phrase, an adjective phrase, or an adverb phrase:

PREMODIFIER	HEADWORD
new high-yielding hybrid	varieties
slightly more	mature
ever so	slowly

preposition

A class of words used with nouns and other words to form prepositional phrases. Prepositions form a small group of, generally, small words. The commonest are:

about	above	across	after
against	along	among	around
as	at	before	behind
below	beneath	beside	between
beyond	but	by	despite
during	except	for	from
in	inside	into	like
near	of	off	on
over	past	round	since
through	throughout	till	to
towards	under	underneath	until
up	upon	with	within
without			

There are also two-, three-, and four-word prepositions:

along with	apart from	as well as	away from
because of	close to	except for	in front of
instead of	in the face of	next to	on to
on top of	out of	owing to	up to

Prepositions come before:

- a noun: **below** ground
- a pronoun: **after** me
- a verbal noun: **without** leaving
- a noun phrase: **during** the last month

Further information

The following entries also contain information about prepositions: **prepositional phase**; **prepositional verb**; **preposition at the end of a sentence**; **preposition stranding**.

P

prepositional phrase

A **phrase** with a **preposition** as its **headword**. The preposition comes at the beginning of the phrase and is followed by:

■ a **noun**

preposition	noun
below	ground

■ a **pronoun**

preposition	pronoun
after	me

■ a **verbal noun**

preposition	verbal noun
without	leaving

■ a **noun phrase**

preposition	noun phrase
during	the last month

Uses

Prepositional phrases have two main uses:

■ to **modify** a noun

When they form part of a noun phrase, they normally come after the noun. (So they are, technically, **postmodifiers**.) For example:

Court actions **in foreign countries**

■ as an **adverbial**

When they are used as adverbials, they give information about:
  place
  time
  manner
  reason
  purpose

prepositional verb

A **verb** that is followed by a **preposition**. Examples are:

We **decided on** the ballet.

Money worries and overwork **led to** illness.

Prepositional verbs may seem similar to **phrasal verbs** like *dig up*, but there is a difference in the way they are constructed and used:

	PREPOSITIONAL VERBS	PHRASAL VERBS
Structure:	**verb + preposition**	**verb + adverb**
Use 1:	**transitive** (*must* be followed by an object)	**transitive** or **intransitive** (doesn't have to be followed by an object)
Use 2:	Sentence cannot be rearranged. We can only say:	Sentence can be rearranged. We can say:
	We **decided on** the ballet. ✓	They've **dug up** a lot of human bones ...
	We cannot say	We can also say:
	We **decided** the ballet on. ✗	They've **dug** a lot of human bones **up** ...

See also: **phrasal verb**.

P

preposition at the end of a sentence

Some people argue that you should never place a preposition at the end of a sentence. They say that the word 'preposition' refers to something that is placed before ('pre-') something else, so it is absurd to place it last in the sentence where it cannot come before anything except a full stop. This opinion is ingenious but completely wrong. Writers have been placing prepositions at the end of sentences for centuries, for the very good reason that this is often the best place for them! It is sometimes possible to reword a sentence so that the preposition does not fall at the end:

These are the shipping lists you asked **for**.

↓

These are the shipping lists **for** which you asked.

But this revised version is more formal and, many would think, a bit pompous. Often such revisions are impossible. For example, it is impossible to rearrange the following so that the preposition does not fall at the end of the sentence:

Another defeat this weekend doesn't bear thinking **about**.

So this is one 'rule' that can safely be ignored.

preposition stranding

Sometimes a **preposition** is separated from the words that normally come after it (its **complement**). For example:

Who did you study with?

In such cases the preposition is described as 'stranded'.

present continuous

A **tense** that is made by using the **present tense** of the verb *to be* with the **present participle** of the main verb:

VERB STEM	PRESENT CONTINUOUS TENSE:
sing	I am singing, she is singing, you are singing, etc.
be	I am being, she is being, etc.

Uses

The commonest uses of this tense are:

■ actions going on now

Councillor Lexa Robinson said: 'I **am speaking** as a parish councillor and as a resident of Craigmore Drive for 25 years.'

■ actions continuing over a period including the present

Many women **are staying** single and breaking away from the traditional rules that kept women in a lower position.

■ actions planned for the future

After school tomorrow **we are leaving** Royal Oak and driving up north.

present participle

A form of the **verb** made by adding *-ing* to the verb stem. (If a verb stem ends in *e*, that letter is removed.)

VERB STEM	PRESENT PARTICIPLE
sing	singing
write	writing

Uses

■ To form **continuous** tenses

	sing	write
present continuous	they are **singing**	they are **writing**
past continuous	they were **singing**	they were **writing**
	... and so on ...	

■ In **non-finite clauses**

These are similar in structure and usage to finite clauses but they contain no finite **auxiliary verb**. Often, too, the **subject** of the clause is missed out. For example:

The men	**working with him**	then walked out.
	non-finite clause	

The words *working with him* are a short form for **who were** *working with him*.

present perfect

A **verb tense** formed by combining the **present tense** of the verb *to have* with the **past participle** of the **main verb**:

SUBJECT	PRESENT TENSE OF 'HAVE'	PAST PARTICIPLE OF MAIN VERB
She	has	worked
They	have	written

Uses

■ To describe an incomplete action or series of actions continuing into the present:

Engel is German by birth but **has lived** in Britain for the last twenty years.

- To describe a past action with results continuing to the present:

    Fire **has damaged** a disused hotel at Abingdon.

- In an adverbial clause of time referring to the future:

    Massive stars will collapse in on themselves when they **have exhausted** their nuclear fuel.

present perfect continuous

A **tense** formed by combining the **present perfect** of the verb *to be* with the **present participle** of the **main verb**:

SUBJECT	PRESENT PERFECT OF 'BE'	PRESENT PARTICIPLE OF MAIN VERB
She	has been	working
They	have been	writing

Uses

- To refer to a repeated or continuous action with effects in the present:

    She **has been working** out in Sierra Leone for a number of years.

- To refer to a fairly recent activity that was repeated or continuous and is relevant now:

    Recently Julia **has been encountering** difficulties.

- To explain something in the present by referring to a past action or event:

    I'm happy with my decision to rest him because he **has been competing** since January.

present tense

This is also called the simple present **tense**. In **regular verbs**, it is formed by using the verb **stem**, which is followed by *s* in the **third person singular**:

	SINGULAR	PLURAL
1st person	I walk	we walk
2nd person	you walk (thou walkest)	you walk
3rd person	he/she/it walks	they walk

Uses

■ Present feelings and thoughts:

  'I **feel** rather sick,' she said.

■ Actions or states that are true now but have no particular reference to time:

  He **lives** in London.

■ Timeless truths and scientific laws:

  Fairly pure water **freezes** at about 0 degrees C.

■ Habitual actions:

  Nearly a quarter of men **clean** out their cars once a month.

■ Open **conditionals**:

  If I **see** anything wrong, I'll ring you later from my surgery.

■ Scheduled future actions:

  The following day, we **travel** to Berlin.

■ Newspaper headlines:

  Ministers **flout** arms sales code

■ Narrative (occasionally):

  And he **says** to her, 'What did you do before you joined the police?'

■ Retelling a story in, for example, a review:

  Enter the Hero, who then **fights** it out with the baddies.

■ In commentaries:

  In it **goes**, but it's too strong for Hasselbank.

primary auxiliary verb

The primary auxiliary verbs are *be*, *do*, and *have*. Auxiliary verbs are used with a **main verb** to form the **verb phrase**:

SUBJECT	PRIMARY AUXILIARY VERB(S)	MAIN VERB
we	**were**	walking
he	**had**	wanted
you	**did**	know

Primary auxiliaries are different from other auxiliary verbs because they can also be used as main verbs. For example:

> In England our weather **is** always abnormal.

> He **has** a plan.

> I **did** a lot of work with business plans.

---

pronoun

A class of words that 'stand in' for other words, usually:

- **nouns**
- **noun phrases**
- other **pronouns**.

Pronouns enable the writer and speaker to avoid long-winded repetitions of things that have already been expressed. (See **pronoun reference**.)

Pronouns fall into seven groups:

- **personal**

The personal pronouns are:

> I/me, we/us, you (thou), he/him, she/her, it, one, they/them

They are used to refer back to nouns which have already been used in the text:

> Machiavelli set out on 17 December 1507. **He** travelled across Lombardy.

- **possessive**

The possessive pronouns are:

> mine, ours, yours, hers, his, its, theirs

They are used in sentences such as:

> My cooking's probably even worse than **yours**.

> Michael Joseph says there has been no breach: 'The *Sunday Times*'s promotion is **theirs**, not **ours**.'

These are true pronouns because they stand alone, without being attached to a noun, by contrast with *my, our*, etc. which always come before a noun and are better referred to as **possessive determiners**.

■ **reflexive**

These are:

> myself, ourselves, yourself, yourselves, himself, herself, itself, oneself, themselves

They are used in sentences such as:

> 'Make **yourselves** comfortable here,' he snapped.

> As we tried to calm **ourselves** with sweet coffee, a Swiss traveller appeared.

■ **demonstrative**

The demonstrative pronouns are:

> this, that, these, those

When these words stand alone, they are pronouns; for example in sentences like this:

> The strong—**those** in powerful Unions—gained at the expense of the weak.

They can also be used before a noun, in which case they are not pronouns but **determiners**:

> **This** decision will cause greater uncertainty.

■ **interrogative**

These are:

> who, whom, whose, what, which

They are used in the formation of questions:

> **Whom** did the King talk to?

■ **relative**

The relative pronouns are:

> who, whom, whose, that, which

They are used to introduce **relative clauses**:

> The artist **who** did my album cover used an airbrush and I got him to do three guitars for me.

■ **indefinite**

This is a large group of pronouns which refer less precisely than the others listed above. They include:

some	someone	somebody	something
any	anyone	anybody	anything
none	no one	nobody	nothing
everyone	everybody	everything	all
either	neither	both	each

For example:

As I keep saying, I don't need you or **anybody** else to tell me what I can or cannot do.

He could hear **nothing**.

Further information

The following entries also contain information about pronouns: **he, she, or it?**; **I/me.**

pronoun reference

In good writing pronouns are used accurately and clearly. In the extract that follows, the pronouns have been highlighted and numbered:

I (1) was met by a minder from the news department, Ian Whitehead, **who** (2) took **me** (3) aside, as **he** (4) was no doubt used to doing with journalists, and told **me** (5) to 'go easy' on His Lordship, **whose** (6) knowledge of Indo-China was limited. With a film camera turning, I began by asking the minister **who** (7) exactly these reasonable Khmer Rouge were. 'Um ...' **he** (8) replied. When **I** (9) asked for their names, Whitehead threw **himself** (10) in front of the camera, yelling, 'Stop **this** (11) now! **This** (12) is not the way **we** (13) were led to believe the line of questioning would go!' No 'line' had been agreed. Nevertheless, **he** (14) refused to allow the interview to proceed until **he** (15) had approved the questions.

	WORD	TYPE OF PRONOUN	REFERS TO
1	I	personal	the writer
2	who	relative	a minder from the news department, Ian Whitehead
3	me	personal (objective)	the writer
4	he	personal	Ian Whitehead
5	me	personal (objective)	the writer
6	whose	relative	His Lordship
7	who	interrogative	these reasonable Khmer Rouge
8	he	personal	the minister
9	I	personal	the writer
10	himself	reflexive	Whitehead
11	this	demonstrative	the journalist's behaviour
12	This	demonstrative	the line of questioning being pursued
13	we	personal	officials at the Foreign Office
14	he	personal	Whitehead
15	he	personal	Whitehead

As the example shows, pronouns do not always refer to specific words or phrases in the text. Sometimes they refer to broader ideas contained in it. For example, the writer quotes Whitehead using 'this' twice to refer to the way in which the minister was being questioned and 'we' to refer to him and his (unnamed) colleagues.

pronunciation

The general term 'pronunciation' covers all aspects of the way in which a speaker produces the sounds that make up a word or longer utterance. Spoken **standard English** consists of 44

phonemes, or speech sounds. How these are actually produced varies from individual to individual, group to group, and region to region. These variations are referred to as **accents**.

Individual words consist of syllables, and in every word of more than one syllable there is a difference of emphasis in the ways in which syllables are sounded. This is known as **stress**. There are stress patterns within whole sentences, too. The meaning of a sentence can also be varied by changing its 'tune', or **intonation**.

proper noun

A group of words that refer to people, places, and things that are unique within the context of the text. In written English they are spelled with an initial capital letter:

Maryland   Shakespeare

Proper nouns can also consist of more than one word:

the New Oxford Dictionary of English   the US Senate

punctuation

Punctuation is part of the way in which we set out written text so that it can be read quickly, easily, and accurately. When we read, our eyes do not move steadily along the line of text reading every letter and every word. Instead, they 'dart' along, taking in small chunks of text as they go. Good punctuation makes this process much easier. It is a set of conventions: we expect it to be used in certain ways to which we have become accustomed. However, these conventions are not completely fixed. Some aspects of punctuation don't change much: the use of full stops (periods) at the end of sentences, for example. Others are more open to variation and can vary from writer to writer, and can change over time. Commas are a case in point.

Punctuation in this guide

There are separate entries for each punctuation point and additional entries dealing with particular applications of punctuation:

▶

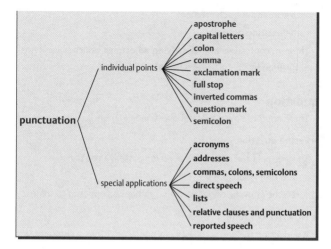

purpose

Adverbials and adverbial clauses can be used to provide information about why things occur—for what purpose they are done.

Adverbials

The commonest type of adverbial used to show purpose is a **prepositional phrase** beginning with *for*:

I've always grown vegetables **for pleasure or necessity**.

Adverbial clauses

Adverbial clauses of purpose often begin with *so that*:

I showed him the car **so that he knew I wasn't lying to him**.

Infinitive clauses are also frequently used for this purpose, introduced by *in order to*, *so as to*, or *just to*:

Someone may grab your collar with both hands **in order to headbutt you in the face**.

qualitative adjective

Adjectives that describe the qualities of a person, thing, or idea. For example:

a **stupendous** achievement

an **exciting** proposal

They are contrasted with **classifying adjectives**, which place items into categories (for example, *annual*, *nuclear*).

question

There are three main types of question in English:

■ yes/no question

These expect the answer *yes* or *no* (or possibly *I don't know*):

Are they good jobs?

Did he know just how deeply his father was opposed to things?

■ either/or question

A variant on the yes/no question is one which offers a choice of response:

Do you want a strong cup or a weak one?

Here the respondent can't answer *yes* or *no*; the only possible responses are *a strong cup*, or *a weak one* (or a refusal to answer).

■ wh- question

These are sometimes described as 'open' questions, because they allow the respondent a freer choice of answer. They begin with one of these words:

who(m)   which   what   when   where   why   how

For example:

Why are you doing this?

Who has the papers?

Not all questions fall into one of these three groups. Sometimes a question is asked using a regular statement pattern:

You have the papers?

We indicate to a reader that it is a question by placing a question mark at the end of the sentence. In speech the voice is raised at the end of sentence, rather than falling as it does at the end of a statement.

See also: **interrogative**; **tag question**.

q

question mark

This punctuation mark is used to mark the end of a question.

What is your name?

It can also be used to indicate that the writer believes that a statement is doubtful or questionable:

All was going well until a passing lad with a sense of fun (?) pulled out the plug.

quite

This **adverb** has a number of uses, and one of the commonest is as a **modifier** before an **adjective** or another adverb. For example:

It is **quite** impossible.

This could happen **quite** rapidly.

As these two examples show, *quite* has two distinct meanings:

- 'completely': *quite impossible*
- 'fairly': *quite rapidly.*

In the following example, the word is used twice, illustrating both meanings:

The defendant stared at her and then **quite** deliberately drove over her, **quite** slowly.

It is important to avoid confusion between the two meanings:

At sixteen Sarah was **quite** beautiful, but she didn't make the most of herself.

Does the writer mean that she was 'very beautiful' or 'fairly beautiful'? It isn't clear.

quotation marks

See **inverted commas**.

reason

Adverbials and adverbial clauses can be used to answer the question *Why?* to provide information about the reason for something happening.

Adverbials

These are often introduced by expressions such as *because of*:

Did the person leave **because of a management failure**?

Adverbial clauses

These are commonly introduced by the **conjunctions** *because*, *since*, and *as*:

Hindley and Catherine were angry **because they had not received any presents**.

It was not difficult for Anne **since she had been encouraged by her father to practise her clog dancing on the kitchen hearth**.

Non-finite clauses are constructed using the **present participle**:

I knew about them **because of being at art college**.

reference

We normally read texts in sequence from beginning to end. (Certain texts, like newspapers and magazines, are more likely to be dipped into and not read in the order in which they are printed. But even with these we usually read individual stories or articles from beginning to end.) Good writers make things easier for their readers by referring back to things that have already been mentioned and forward to things that will be mentioned later. This gives a text cohesion.

There are three main types of reference: **ellipsis**, **referring words**, and **sentence adverbials**.

See also: **paragraph**; **pronoun reference**.

referring words

Words like **pronouns** which help us to refer clearly and briefly to what has gone before, or what is coming after, without unnecessary repetition. The main types of referring word are:

- pronouns

  personal (I, she, etc.)
  demonstrative (this, those, etc.)
  relative (who(m), which, etc.).

- **determiners**

  For example, *all three* in the following text:

  > I remember asking Sir Alfred Beit to lend his famous Vermeer and two great paintings by Metsu. He refused but while our exhibition was on at the Academy, **all three** paintings were stolen from his home …

- other words and phrases

  For example:

  former   latter   above   below

  See also: **pronoun reference**.

reflexive pronoun

The reflexive pronouns are:

myself, ourselves, yourself, yourselves, himself, herself, itself, oneself, themselves

They are used in sentences such as:

'Make **yourselves** comfortable here,' he snapped.

As we tried to calm **ourselves** with sweet coffee, a Swiss traveller appeared.

regular verb

A **verb** that follows this pattern:

	PRESENT TENSE	PAST TENSE	PAST PARTICIPLE
walk	I walk / she walks	walked	walked
stem	stem (+ -s)	stem + -ed (or + -d, if stem ends with e)	stem + -ed (or + -d, if stem ends with e)

See also: **irregular verb**.

relative adverb

An **adverb** that is used to introduce a **relative clause**. The relative adverbs are:

when   where   why

In the following examples the relative adverb is in bold and the relative clause in italics:

You were six that year ***when*** *Henry died.*

It's been very strange filming in the place ***where*** *I spent my formative years.*

There are all sorts of reasons ***why*** *people haven't contributed to a pension scheme.*

relative clause

A **clause** that does a similar job to an **adjective**:

It's a **clever** crowd-pleaser. (adjective)

It's a crowd-pleaser **that knows how to press all the right buttons**. (relative clause)

Relative clauses are used as **postmodifiers** in noun phrases and are introduced by one of the **relative pronouns**:

who   whom   whose   which   that

Sometimes the relative pronoun is missed out:

Could you be the person **they're looking for**?

This could also be written:

Could you be the person **whom they're looking for**?

In their full form relative clauses are like mini-sentences. You can remove them from the sentence they are in and, with very few changes, turn them into sentences in their own right:

ORIGINAL	TWO-SENTENCE VERSION
It's a crowd-pleaser that knows how to press all the right buttons.	It's a crowd-pleaser. It knows how to press all the right buttons.

Non-finite relative clauses are also common:

VERB FORM	SAMPLE SENTENCE	EQUIVALENT USING FINITE VERB
Infinitive	That's the way **to say it**.	That's the way that you should say it.
Present participle	The woman **talking** has raised a large family.	The woman who is talking has raised a large family.
Past participle	That's a picture **taken from a helicopter or an aeroplane**.	That's a picture that was taken from a helicopter or an aeroplane.

relative clauses and punctuation

In written English the difference between **defining** and **non-defining relative clauses** is highlighted by punctuation. Non-defining relative clauses are enclosed by commas:

The minister, who had red hair and fire in his eye, started on an upbeat note.

Defining relative clauses are not enclosed by commas:

A person who is mentally handicapped is just as much a member of society as anyone else.

relative pronoun

Relative pronouns are used to introduce **relative clauses**. The relative pronouns are:

who   whom   whose   which   that

It is also possible to introduce certain relative clauses without the use of a relative pronoun—the **zero relative**.

reported speech

In reports and stories it is often necessary to tell the reader what someone has said. If the words are quoted exactly as spoken, it is **direct speech**. In writing, this is shown by the use of punctuation. In reported speech the actual words are not quoted, but are usually summed up. For example:

1. Both students and lecturers said that they felt that lectures gave an opportunity for personal contact.
2. PC Clifford would have welcomed the tea, but said that he must get back to the scene of the tragedy.

These two examples show two different forms of reported speech.

Generalizing and summarizing

In (1) the writer has summed up what was said. Presumably a number of different people said different things, but all in all they agreed that lectures gave an opportunity for personal contact. Sometimes a writer summarizes even more briefly:

He expressed his concern for the workforce and their families.

Reporting the words

In example (2) the writer is clearly much closer to the actual words used. The police officer probably said something like, 'I must get back to the scene of the tragedy', although he may not have used those exact words. The extensive quotation of actual words is comparatively rare in reported speech; generalizing and summarizing are much more common.

Verb tense

Stories and reports are normally written using past tenses. This means that the words of reported speech should also be put in the past tense. If someone says, 'I am going to work', it is reported as *He said that he was going to work*. What happens is that each verb is shifted back in time:

go	becomes	went
is	become	was
will	becomes	would

and so on.

Similarly, time **adverbials** have to be changed:

now	becomes	then
today	become	that day
yesterday	becomes	the day before

and so on.

Personal pronouns, too, have to shift from first person to third:

I		he/she
us	becomes	them
you		they

and so on.

So, for example:

'At the moment I'm staying with a friend in Peckham,' he said, 'but next week I shall be moving into my own flat.'

becomes:

He said that at the time he was staying with a friend in Peckham, but that the following week he would be moving into his own flat.

restrictive relative clause

Another name for a **defining relative clause**.

result

Adverbial clauses can be used to show the result of an action or situation described in the main clause:

My father threatened to punish them, **so they were forced to accept my company**. (action)

The two metal coffee jugs were so hot **that Cormack dropped them with a yelp**. (situation)

Result clauses can be introduced by:

so	and so	so that
so ... that	such (a) ... that	in such a way that

root

What is left when you remove all prefixes and suffixes from a word:

WORD	PREFIXES AND SUFFIXES	ROOT
misunderstanding	mis-, under-, -ing	stand
inspirational	in-, -ation-, -al	spir

Sometimes the root may be a word in its own right, like *stand*, but often, like *spir*, it is not. (But the root *spir*, which is Latin in origin, occurs in other words such as *aspired*, *transpiration*, and *expire*.

second person

You (and, in some dialects, *thou/thee*). It is a term used when talking about the **present tense** of **verbs** and personal **pronouns**.

---

semicolon

Semicolons are used to mark a break between two parts of a sentence. Usually the two parts that are separated in this way could stand as sentences in their own right. You use a semicolon because you want to show that there is a close link between them:

> He loved chasing women, but did not like them; it was the chase that excited him. ✓

If you write this as two separate sentences, you change the meaning slightly by increasing the separation between the two ideas:

> He loved chasing women, but did not like them. It was the chase that excited him. ✓

Some writers try to use a **comma** instead of a semicolon for this purpose. This is a mistake. The comma is weaker and when we are reading it does not 'stop' the eye in the same way as a semicolon:

> He loved chasing women, but did not like them, it was the chase that excited him. ✗

The 'comma splice', as this is called, is best avoided.

Lists

If a list contains items that are quite long, semicolons can be used instead of commas to separate them:

> Weeds may reach the lawn in various ways: as seeds blown by the wind; carried by birds; brought in on muddy footwear, machinery, or tools; or concealed in unsterilized soil or badly made compost used for top-dressing.

See also: **commas, colons, and semicolons**.

semivowel

The speech sounds which begin the words *we* and *you* are referred to as semivowels.

sentence

A unit of language consisting of one or more **finite clauses**. If a sentence contains just one clause, it is described as **simple**:

> The commissioners entered Pisa on Friday 8 June.

> Surrounded by high waves, in the middle of the North Sea, a team of French engineers are constructing the first offshore oil-rig platforms.

As the second of the examples shows, simple sentences are not necessarily either short, or simple in meaning.

If a sentence contains more than one finite clause it is described as **multiple**. In the example that follows the clauses have been separated:

> Nobody is sure   whether it will work   but everything
>   has to be done
>   fast.

Multiple sentences can be either **compound** or **complex**.

Sentence types

Sentences can follow one of four patterns according to their communicative purpose.

■ **Declarative**

Declarative sentences are used to make statements.

> Success at every level always does wonders for everyone.

■ **Exclamative**

Exclamative sentences are used in exclamations.

> What a difference a day makes!

■ **Imperative**

Imperative sentences are used to make commands.

Give me the idiots' version.

■ Interrogative

Interrogative sentences are used to ask questions.

How did this happen?

There are three main types of question: **either/or questions**, **wh-questions**, and **yes/no questions**. There is also a special type of question added at the end of a sentence: the **tag question**.

Further information

The information given above is summed up in the diagram below. Each of the words in bold type has its own entry, where further information can be found.

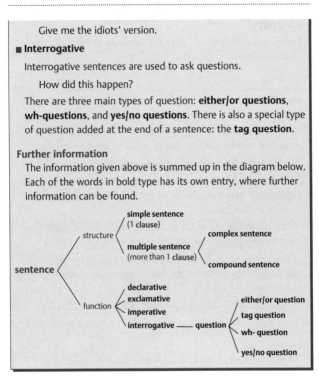

sentence adverbial

An **adverbial** used in a piece of continuous writing to show the links between different sections, or to provide a comment by the author:

■ **conjuncts** make links

■ **disjuncts** provide comments.

Each has its own entry where it is covered in more detail.
See also: **paragraph**.

shall

A **modal auxiliary verb** used in the formation of future tenses:

simple future	I/we shall see
future continuous	I/we shall be seeing
future perfect	I/we shall have seen
future perfect continuous	I/we shall have been seeing

As these examples demonstrate, *shall* is normally used for the **first person** (*I* and *we*). But *will* is frequently used instead of *shall*: see **will/shall**.

should

A **modal auxiliary verb** used to refer to possible events in the future:

I **should** be there before then.

It is also used to express that something is desirable:

He said that they **should** see a speech therapist.

simple aspect

The verb **aspect** which contrasts with the **continuous aspect**. It can be:

■ present

The kiosks are the most agreeable buildings that the Turks have: they **build** some on the seashore and by riversides, but foremost in the gardens near the fountains ....

For more information on this, see **present tense**.

■ past

Few would claim that US industrialists were thinking in military terms when they **built** this country's railway system, but their work still affected the course of the Civil War.

For more information on this, see **past tense**.

■ future

Once 44% of the money is in, a Swiss construction firm will build 'luxury Mediterranean-style homes' on the sites.

For more information on this, see **future tense**.

S

simple future tense

See **future tense**.

simple past tense

See **past tense**.

simple present tense

See **present tense**.

simple sentence

See **sentence**.

since

Conjunction

A **subordinating conjunction** used to introduce two types of **adverbial clause**:

■ **time**

> **Since** we moved here the asthma has got worse.

■ **reason**

> The Germans thought Danzig might be bombed but not Gdynia, **since** the latter is a Polish city.

Preposition

It is also used as a preposition:

> I haven't seen her **since** Monday.

singular

See **number**.

slang

A form of the language that is not **standard English**. Different social groups often use a special vocabulary. Sometimes this is fairly widespread and well understood. In the sentences that follow, the slang expressions are in bold type.

But Doreen was **a dab hand** at computers.

If Martin is prepared to take the risk, he could be **quids in**.

I just wanted to be sure you weren't trying to **pull a fast one** on me.

Some slang is confined to small tightly-knit groups who can use it to exclude outsiders. Slang is by definition informal and non-standard. It is also often sexual or scatological.

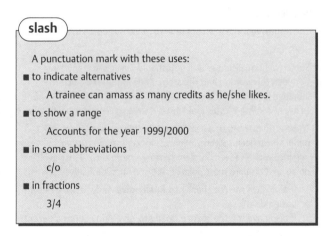

slash

A punctuation mark with these uses:

■ to indicate alternatives

   A trainee can amass as many credits as he/she likes.

■ to show a range

   Accounts for the year 1999/2000

■ in some abbreviations

   c/o

■ in fractions

   3/4

spelling

English spelling causes problems for two main reasons:

■ There are more sounds in the language than letters with which to express them. Although there are only five **vowel** letters (six, if you include *y*) there are over twenty vowel sounds. So each vowel letter has to work overtime to accommodate this variety. The letter *a*, for example, has to express the two different sounds in these words:

   hat
   hate

> ■ Spelling has evolved at a different speed and in different ways
> from pronunciation. This accounts for the bizarre variety of ways
> in which the letters 'ough' are used: *cough*, *dough*, *through*,
> *thorough*, etc.
>
> See also: **consonant**; **digraph**; **grapheme**.

split infinitive

The **infinitive** is the form of the **verb** made by adding *to* to its **stem**:

to go

Some traditionalists say that you should never place anything
between the word *to* and the stem. They argue that since the
infinitive is a part of the verb it should never be split. So it is wrong
to say *to boldly go*. You should instead say *to go boldly* or *boldly to go*.

There is no grammatical justification for this so-called 'rule' and
people have been splitting infinitives for centuries. Splitting an
infinitive with an adverb frequently sounds more natural than avoiding
doing so. Compare these pairs of split and unsplit infinitives:

It also gave me the chance **to finally give** Andy Serkis a decent
screen death.
It also gave me the chance **finally to give** Andy Serkis a decent
screen death.
Do you feel under any pressure **to actually move** to LA full-time?
Do you feel under any pressure **actually to move** to LA full-time?
I don't think she did it **to consciously make** me a better ski racer.
I don't think she did it **consciously to make** me a better ski racer.

In each case the split version reads more easily than the unsplit.

Sometimes it is actually impossible to convey your meaning unless
you do split an infinitive. This is particularly true of adverbs such as
really. For example:

Everyone else thought they were too young **to really cope** with
adult responsibilities.

If you move *really* to another position you change the meaning and/
or emphasis of the sentence:

Everyone else thought they were too young **really** to cope with adult responsibilities.

Everyone else thought they were too young to cope **really** with adult responsibilities.

standard English

The form of English that is most widely understood across the country. In different regions and social classes different **dialects** may be used. This means that it is sometimes difficult for a person from one region to understand what is being said by a person from another; a Cornish person, for example, may struggle to understand what is said by a Glaswegian or a Tynesider. This is not just a matter of **accent**; each dialect has its own distinctive vocabulary and variations of grammar. The problem can be overcome if both speakers can also use standard English. This is the version of English which is described by grammars and other books about language (although some also describe national or regional variations). Expressions and constructions that differ from it are described as 'non-standard'.

stem

The base form of the **verb**. In regular verbs all the other forms of the verb are constructed using the stem:

stem	walk
infinitive	to walk
present tense	walk/walks
present participle	walking
past tense	walked
past participle	walked

S

stress

An element of **pronunciation**. There are two types of stress:

■ word stress

■ sentence stress.

Word stress

This occurs in any word of more than one **syllable**. In polysyllabic words one syllable is spoken with more emphasis than the others. In the following list the stressed syllable is printed in bold type:

happy   de**nied**   **cel**ery   suc**cess**ful

Words with three or more syllables will often also have a syllable that carries secondary stress: it is also stressed, but not as much as the main stressed syllable. In the following words it is printed in italic type:

exa*mi***na**tion   *repre***sent**ative

Sentence stress

There is also a pattern of **primary** and *secondary* stress within **phrases**, **clauses**, and **sentences**:

They *wanted* to sell us their **house**.

This fairly regular conversational stress can be altered to make a particular emphasis. For example:

They wanted to sell us **their** house.

structure word

The vocabulary of English can be divided into content words and structure words. Structure words are:

- **conjunctions**
- **prepositions**
- **pronouns**
- **determiners**.

Whereas content words generally have a meaning that you can look up in a dictionary, structure words are the 'glue' that hold content words together in a sentence. If you look them up in a dictionary you will not be offered a meaning, but an explanation of how they are used.

S

subject

In a statement **clause**, the subject:

- comes at or near the beginning of the clause
- comes before the **verb**
- agrees with the verb in **number** and **person**
- often also gives an indication of what the clause is about.

The subject can be:

■ **a noun**

> **Yoga** is religious.

■ **a verbal noun**

> **Dancing** is a wonderful way of keeping in training.

■ **an infinitive**

> **To err** is human.

■ **a pronoun**

> **They** argued ferociously about Ireland.

■ **a noun phrase**

> **The core of the problems** is simple.

■ **a noun clause**

> **What he said** was true.

subject complement

Part of a **clause** that completes the **subject**. In a statement clause it comes after the **verb** and refers to the same person, thing, or idea as the subject. For example:

SUBJECT	VERB	SUBJECT COMPLEMENT
My job	is	very unusual.
Alton man Giles Stogdon	will become	the new police chief for Winchester.

The verb in sentences like this works in a similar way to an equal sign:

> My job = very unusual.

A subject complement can be:

■ **a noun**

> Cash is **king**.

■ a **pronoun**

> It was **you**!

■ a **numeral**

> I was **third**.

■ a **noun phrase**

> Alton man Giles Stogdon will become **the new police chief for Winchester**.

■ an **adjective** or **adjective phrase**

> My job is **very unusual**.

subjective case

See **case**.

subjunctive

The subjunctive is one of three **moods**, the others being the indicative and the **imperative**. The subjunctive can be present or past.

Present subjunctive

This is the same as the verb **stem**. It is most commonly used in **clauses** beginning with *that* to express wishes or commands:

> In any event Mr Poon would prefer that the jury **see** the video.

Past subjunctive

This is limited to the verb *were*, used in place of *was*. This is most commonly used in conditional clauses where the condition is viewed as unlikely:

> If he **were** only a little nicer, then nobody would fear him.

or impossible:

> If I **were** you I'd hide all the sharp objects in your house.

subordinate clause

A **clause** that grammatically forms part of a **main clause**. In a
complex sentence there is one main clause and one (or more)
clauses that depend on it. If you break the sentence into its separate
clauses you usually find that the main clause will still stand up if you
replace the other clause(s) with a single word:

	MAIN CLAUSE	SUBORDINATE CLAUSE
complex sentence	The problem is	**that grasses are difficult to contain.**
simple sentence	The problem is **weeds.**	

The main clause can follow one of the seven standard patterns.
Within the structure of the main clause, subordinate clauses can act
as:

■ **subject**

  What I want to do now is to look at two elements.

■ **object**

  Describe **how the accident happened**.

■ **subject complement**

  The problem is **that despite holding all those top jobs down
  the years, Cicutto's media profile was virtually non-existent**.

■ **object complement**

  They had made him **what he was**.

■ **adverbial**

  We'll talk about it **when we meet this evening**.

In each case the subordinate clause can be replaced by a single word
or a short phrase, without changing the grammar of the main
clause:

  My aim is to look at two elements.

  Describe **the accident**.

  The problem is **Cicutto's feeble media profile**.

S

They had made him **a hero**.

We'll talk about it **later**.

subordinating conjunction

A **conjunction** used to introduce a **subordinate clause**. Examples are:

when	how	where	why
if	although	unless	since
because	until	so	as

suffix

Part of a **word** that comes after the **base**. In the list of words that follows, the suffixes are printed in bold type:

child**ish**   king**dom**   pictur**esque**

Suffixes make a new word out of the base. They often also change it from one **word class** to another. So, for example, the noun *child* becomes the adjective *childish*.

Verb suffixes

SUFFIX	EXAMPLE	BASE
-ify	beautify	beauty
-ise/-ize	idolize	idol

Adjective suffixes

SUFFIX	EXAMPLE	BASE
-able/-ible	excitable	excite
-al/-ial	adverbial	adverb
-ate	insensate	sense
-ed	flat-roofed	flat roof
-esque	picturesque	picture
-ful	fateful	fate
-ic	Icelandic	Iceland
-ical	economical	economy
-ish	childish	child
-ive	plaintive	plaint
-less	childless	child

SUFFIX	EXAMPLE	BASE
-like	blood-like	blood
-ous	analagous	analogy
-y	dozy	doze

Adverb suffixes

SUFFIX	EXAMPLE	BASE
-ly	happily	happy
-ward(s)	westwards	west
-wise	clockwise	clock

Noun suffixes

SUFFIX	EXAMPLE	BASE
-age	acreage	acre
-al	referral	refer
-ant/-ent	inhabitant	inhabit
-ation/-ion	examination	examine
-dom	kingdom	king
-ee	addressee	address
-eer	auctioneer	auction
-er	abstainer	abstain
-ess	tigress	tiger
-ery	scenery	scene
-ette	leatherette	leather
-ful	handful	hand
-hood	neighbourhood	neighbour
-ing	mooring	moor
-ism	impressionism	impression
-ist	pianist	piano
-ity	chastity	chaste
-ment	postponement	postpone
-ness	happiness	happy
-ocracy	meritocracy	merit
-or	director	direct
-ship	directorship	director
-ster	trickster	trick

S

superlative

Many **adjectives** can have three forms:

ABSOLUTE	COMPARATIVE	SUPERLATIVE
small	smaller	smallest
attractive	more attractive	most attractive

The comparative form is used when comparing two items; the superlative is used when there are more than two:

> She is **smaller** than her brother. (comparative)

> The **smallest** of the three specialist colleges, it has just over 150 full-time students, of whom about half come from Wales. (superlative)

The superlative is formed in different ways according to the length of the base adjective. If it has one syllable, then the letters *-est* are added. If the word has three syllables or more then the word *most* is added before the adjective: *most attractive*. Words of two syllables vary: some add *-est* and some use *most*. Some even do both, for example *clever → cleverest/most clever*.

Some adjectives are used to place nouns into groups or categories, for example, *nuclear* and *annual*. These **classifying adjectives** do not have a comparative or superlative form. For example, you cannot talk about

> the **most annual** concert ✗

syllable

English words consist of one or more syllables. Each syllable always contains one speech **vowel**. This may have one or more speech **consonants** before and/or after it. In the examples that follow, the words are broken into syllables:

1 syllable	yacht	house	a
2 syllables	hap-py	lang-uage	prac-tice
3 syllables	bi-cy-cle	sen-si-ble	ac-cid-ent

synonym

A word that has the same or similar meaning to another. The following pairs of words are synonyms:

still	motionless
melody	tune
birth control	contraception
sluggish	lethargic
loud	noisy

syntax

The study of how words are selected and arranged to form sentences. A major part of grammar, the other being **morphology**.

tag question

A question 'tagged on' to the end of a statement. For example:

1. Those daffodils have gone pale, **haven't they**?

2. She shouldn't have left, **should she**?

3. You thought it was still six, **didn't you**?

When a speaker uses a tag question, he or she normally expects agreement or confirmation from the listener.

Structure

■ If the statement contains an **auxiliary verb** the tag question repeats this, as in the first two examples above.

■ If the statement verb is in the simple present or the simple past then the tag question uses *do* or *did*, as in the last example.

■ If the speaker expects the answer 'Yes', then the tag question is in the negative (as in the first and last examples).

■ If the answer 'No' is expected, then the tag question is in the positive, as in the second example.

Pronunciation

Tag questions can be made confidently. In this case they are spoken with falling intonation. If the speaker is more tentative then they are spoken with a rising tone.

s

t

tense

tense

In the terminology of modern grammar, English only has two tenses, **past** and **present**:

VERB	PRESENT TENSE	PAST TENSE
walk	walk/walks	walked
write	write/writes	wrote

Many people are surprised to be told that English has no future tense—and for everyday purposes it isn't a particularly helpful way of describing how English verbs work.

In many ways it is more useful to talk about the whole **verb phrase** and to look at the way it gives information about **time** and **aspect**. If we do this, we can say that English has the following tenses:

	SIMPLE	CONTINUOUS	PERFECT	PERFECT CONTINUOUS
PAST	I walked	I was walking	I had walked	I had been walking
PRESENT	I walk	I am walking	I have walked	I have been walking
FUTURE	I shall/will walk	I shall/will be walking	I shall/will have walked	I shall/will have been walking

As this table shows, the verb phrase in a sentence provides two different types of information:

Time
It tells us whether an event happened in the past or present, or is yet to happen in the future.

Aspect
It also provides information about how the speaker regards any action communicated by the verb. Each of the following verb phrases refers to the present:

I walk (**simple present**)

I am walking (**present continuous**)

I have walked (**present perfect**)

I have been walking (**present perfect continuous**)

But it is obvious that they refer to the present in different ways.

■ The simple present has a range of uses which include eternal truths:

Fairly pure water **freezes** at about 0 degrees C.

and regular or habitual actions:

Nearly a quarter of men **clean** out their cars once a month.

■ The present continuous, on the other hand, places more emphasis on an action that continues over a period of time:

'I **am speaking** from the home of Mrs Browning,' I said.

■ If we use the present perfect, we place yet another emphasis—on the fact that a completed action still has some importance to the present moment:

But the Government **has said** public money will not be available for at least 15 years.

The Government said it in the past, but this is still important at the time of speaking; in a sense the 'saying' is still going on because the Government has apparently not changed its mind.

■ We can even combine the perfect and continuous aspects:

Labour's deputy leader **has been saying** to the councils, 'You may not get as much as you want, but you will certainly get more.'

He has said this to the councils over a period of time; it was in the past but is still important at the time of speaking.

This combination of time and aspect makes it possible to communicate a wide range of different meanings.

Further information

The information given above is summed up in the diagram below. Each of the words in bold type has its own entry, where further information can be found.

t

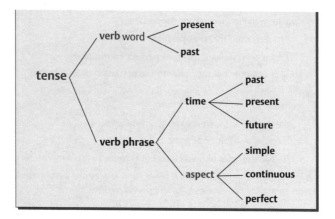

that/which/who(m)

These are the three commonest **relative pronouns** used to introduce **relative clauses**. *Who(m)* is used to refer to people. *That* can be used to refer to people or things, while *which* is only used to refer to things. The main differences between *that* and *which* can be set out like this:

USE	THAT	WHICH
To refer to people	quite common (along with *who(m)*)	almost never
To introduce a **defining** **relative clause**	very common	less common
To introduce a **non-defining** **relative clause**	almost never	nearly always (except referring to people, when *who(m)* is used
Formal writing	less common	more common
Informal writing	more common	less common

t

theirs

A possessive pronoun (see **case**; **possession**). It is sometimes written with an apostrophe (*their's*). This is not **standard English**.

third person

He, *she*, *it*, and *they*. It is a term used when talking about the **present tense** of **verbs** and **personal pronouns**.

time

There are two main ways of indicating time in English sentences: **verb tense**, and the use of **adverbials** and **adverbial clauses**.

Verb tense

The form of the verb phrase gives information about when an action occurred (time) and how the speaker regards it (**aspect**). This is covered in detail in the entry for **tense**.

Adverbials

Adverbials are a common way of indicating when something happened. They may be:

■ **adverbs**

'How are you feeling?' asked Michael **afterwards**.

Common time adverbs are:

afterwards	already	daily	earlier
ever	finally	first	frequently
hourly	immediately	last	later
monthly	never	next	now
often	presently	seldom	shortly
sometimes	soon	still	suddenly
then	today	tomorrow	usually
weekly	yearly	yesterday	yet

■ **adverb phrases**

These are phrases built up on an adverb headword, such as:

shortly afterwards   almost daily   much earlier

t

For example:

> **Much later** I asked, 'Do you still miss Simon a lot?'

■ prepositional phrases

> D. Long will report back **after the Tokyo meeting**.

Prepositional phrases used as time adverbials often begin with:

after	at	before	by	during
for	from	in	on	since
throughout	to	until		

Adverbial clauses

Adverbial clauses of time are introduced by **subordinating conjunctions** including:

| after | as | before | since |
| until | when | while | |

They can be used to describe events that happen:

■ before the event in the main clause:

> **When they heard the news**, they issued statements.

■ at the same time as the event in the main clause:

> **While this was being done**, Byrne and Phillips went off on a recce down to the road.

■ after the event in the main clause:

> It came out of the blue, **before he knew he was famous**.

Tense and adverbials working together

While tense and adverbials can work on their own to indicate time, more often they work together:

We	started	the contract	in April of last year.
	↓		↓
	past tense		adverbial

Sometimes, however, tense and time adverbials can seem to work against each other. The **present continuous tense** can be combined with adverbials of time to refer to the future as well as the present:

The firm **is working** on that standard now.

Later on in the year she **is travelling** to South Africa to visit her daughter Michelle.

The simple present tense can be used for an even wider range of times:

I **place** a teabag and some powdered milk into the enamel cup and then pour on the water and stir with a twig. (present)

Tomorrow night we **travel** to Potosi. (future)

'I want to talk to him,' he **says** to the guard at the door. (past)

My mum and dad **go** there every year. (past, present, and future)

transitive verb

A **verb** that takes an **object**:

subject	verb	object
They	hit	the crossbar.

Some verbs are usually transitive. For example:

admire	avoid	buy	complete	cover	create
cut	damage	demand	destroy	discover	enjoy
expect	find	get	give	hit	keep
like	love	make	mean	need	own
prefer	produce	raise	receive	remove	risk
seek	take	use	want	wear	

Other verbs can be transitive but also **intransitive** (i.e. they do not take an object). An example is the verb *run*:

He **ran** a successful wine business in Marylebone. (transitive)

I just left my car and **ran**. (intransitive)

Ditransitive verbs

Some transitive verbs have two objects, a direct object and an **indirect object**:

We	gave	them	an early Christmas present.
She	told	me	the story.
subject	**verb**	**indirect object**	**direct object**

These verbs are referred to as 'ditransitive' and include:

| bring | buy | give | promise |
| send | show | teach | tell |

uncountable noun

Countable nouns have both a singular and a plural form. Most nouns are countable, because they refer to things that can be counted. By contrast, a small number of nouns do not regularly have a plural form and are called uncountable. Examples include:

mud   snow   butter

In addition, many **abstract nouns** are normally uncountable. For example:

unhappiness   dread   darkness

See also: **countable and uncountable nouns**.

unique

This word is a **classifying adjective**. Classifying adjectives put things into groups or classes so they cannot normally be **modified** by having **adverbs** such as *very* placed in front of them. *Unique* means 'of which there is only one', so it is, strictly speaking, wrong to say, for example:

He was a **very unique** person. ✗

And the following example is doubly absurd:

Almost the most unique residential site along the South Coast. ✗

On the other hand there are a small number of modifiers that can be used with *unique*. The most obvious is *almost*:

Britain is **almost unique** in continuing to charge almost all its domestic customers on an unmeasured basis. [for water] ✓

u

This can be justified because it means that Britain is not the only country to do this; there are a few others.

There is, however, a looser meaning frequently given (especially in informal speech and writing) to *unique*: 'outstanding or remarkable'. When it is used in this sense it is often preceded by *very*:

> A **very unique** 'Town' house situated a stone's throw away from the River Thames and Oxford City Centre.

This use is best avoided in formal speech or writing.

verb

In grammar the word 'verb' is used in two separate but linked ways:

■ to refer to a **word class**

It describes a particular word class in the same way as 'noun', 'preposition', and 'adjective' do.

■ to refer to a **clause element**

It describes a part of a clause in the same way that 'subject', 'object', and 'complement' do. In this sense it is also sometimes called the verb phrase.

Verbs as a word class: types
There are two types of verb: **main** and **auxiliary**.

■ Main verbs: meaning

Main verbs are used for three main purposes:

- to express an action

> She **fled** upstairs to the bathroom.

- to express a state

> She **slept** noiselessly.

- to link the subject with its complement

> She **was** alone.

■ Main verbs: grammar

In grammar verbs are grouped according to what comes after them:

- **transitive verbs**
- **ditransitive verbs**
- **intransitive verbs**
- **linking verbs**.

■ Auxiliary verbs

These are used with main verbs to form a verb phrase (see below). They are of two types: primary and modal.

The **primary auxiliaries** are *be*, *have*, and *do*.

The **modal verbs** include *will*, *shall*, *can*, *may*, *ought*, and *should*.

Verbs as a word class: forms

Verbs can be regular or irregular and have the following forms:

stem	walk	swim	be
infinitive	to walk	to swim	to be
present tense	walk/walks	swim/swims	am/is/are
present participle	walking	swimming	being
past tense	walked	swam	was/were
past participle	walked	swum	been

Verbs as a clause element

In a statement **clause**, the verb normally comes after the **subject** and before the **object** or **complement**. The verb element in a clause can consist of one word or several. Either way it is more correctly referred to as the verb phrase (or sometimes the verb string).

The verb in a clause may be **finite** or **non-finite**. If finite it should **agree** with the **subject** in **number** and **person**.

The verb phrase can be in one of several **tenses**, which express both **time** and **aspect**.

Further information

The information given above is summed up in the diagram below. Each of the words in bold type has its own entry, where further information can be found. ▶

V

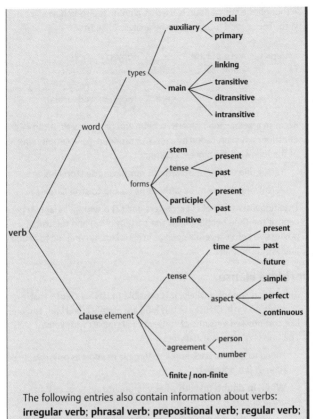

The following entries also contain information about verbs:
irregular verb; phrasal verb; prepositional verb; regular verb; split infinitive; verbal noun.

verbal noun

The *-ing* form of the **verb** used as a **noun**. It is also called a 'gerund'. For example:

Smoking is not permitted.

I don't like **eating** a lot late at night.

Not one day went by without our **having** to stop filming.

Although the verbal noun is used as a noun, it also behaves like a verb. The second example can be analysed like this:

subject	verb phrase		object	
I	don't like	eating	a lot	late at night.
		verb	object	adverbial

Because a verbal noun is partly a noun and partly a verb, it can raise questions when preceded by a noun or pronoun. For example, which of the following sentences is correct?

1. Not one day went by without **our** having to stop filming.

2. Not one day went by without **us** having to stop filming.

Traditionalists say that (1) is correct and (2) is wrong. In fact 90 per cent of the time people follow the pattern of (2) and the use of a possessive before a verbal noun as in (1) is largely confined to fiction and formal writing.

verbless clause

Although it sounds unlikely, it is possible to have a **clause** that contains no **verb**. Clauses of this kind are usually **adverbial**, and are like compressed versions of conventional clauses with verbs. The 'missing' verb is usually *be*:

I need to get you back home to Virginia **as soon as possible**. (= *as soon as it is possible*)

When in doubt, go with what your heart tells you. (= *When you are in doubt*)

Johnson, **though over age**, was allowed to enlist in the Corps. (= *though he was over age*)

Then blend for about 40 seconds or **until smooth**. (= *until it is smooth*)

verb phrase

See **verb**.

verb string

See **verb**.

vocabulary

See **lexis**.

---

voice

English verbs have two voices:

■ active

   I **shot** the sheriff.

■ passive

   The sheriff **was shot** by me.

See also: **active voice**; **passive voice**.

---

vowel

A word with two meanings:

In writing

The five letters: a e i o u

In speech

Vowels are sounds made with the mouth open and the airway
unobstructed (by contrast with consonants where the flow of air is
briefly obstructed in some way). The exact number of vowels depends
on regional accent, but there are more than twenty English vowels.

who/whom

Relative clauses can be introduced by these **relative pronouns**:

   who/whom/whose   which   that

The choice between *who* and *whom* can sometimes cause problems.
The traditional rules are these:

■ use *who* as the subject of the verb:

   Any members **who** find themselves in the Adelaide area can be
   assured of a warm welcome there.

■ use *whom* as the object of the verb:

   Kelith had, once, been my friend **whom** I trusted with all I had …

V

W

■ use *whom* after prepositions:

> To **whom** have you complained?

These rules should still be followed in formal writing. Increasingly, however, *who* is replacing *whom* in speech and less formal writing. For example:

> They had to say **who** they supported.

instead of

> They had to say **whom** they supported.

And

> Currently, most people won't go and see a band **who** they haven't heard of.

instead of

> Currently, most people won't go and see a band of **whom** they haven't heard.

who's/whose

These two are sometimes confused.

■ *Who's* is the contracted form of *who is* or *who has*.

> Doctors said last night Watson, 27, **who's** suffering head injuries, was progressing slowly.

■ *Whose* is the possessive form of *who* and means 'belonging to whom'.

> **Whose** house was it, anyway?

A fairly common error is to use *who's* instead of *whose*:

> Outside the camp the Commander approached the dark-clad figure **who's** cloak was billowing in the wind. ✗

wh- question

A question introduced by a question word:

| who | whom | whose | which | what |
| when | where | why | how | |

For example:

> **Why** are you doing this?
> **Who** has the papers?

This type of question allows a wide range of possible answers and is often referred to as an 'open' question.

will

A **modal auxiliary verb** used:

■ to refer to possible events in the future:

At 59, he **will** be the oldest coach in the First Division.

■ to ask someone to do something:

'**Will** you take Donald for a little walk, Christine?' her mother asked her when she came home from school one afternoon.

■ to show determination:

'He **will** be disciplined,' he said flatly.

■ to volunteer or show willingness:

He **will** not reveal their names without permission.

■ to describe a person's habits (usually undesirable):

Your mother **will** do that.

will/shall

The traditional grammar rules are:

■ use *shall* with *I* and *we*.
■ use *will* with all other **persons**.
■ reverse this for emphasis:

The sea **shall** not have them.

Increasingly, however, *will* is used across the board. *Shall* is by far the least common modal auxiliary verb; in conversation *will* is used fourteen times more frequently than *shall*, despite the frequency that *I* occurs in speech. The only occasion when *shall* is commonly used with *I* and *we* is in questions:

Shall I come with you?

word

One of six grammatical levels, the others being text, **sentence**, **clause**, **phrase**, and **morpheme**. Words are grouped into **word classes** according to their grammatical function. There are four open classes which consist of:

- **adjectives**
- **adverbs**
- **nouns**
- **verbs**.

These classes are known as 'open' because they are still being added to as new words are coined. They are also referred to as **content words**, because they 'contain' meanings which can be defined (as in a dictionary).

There are also four closed classes, to which no new words are added:

- **conjunctions**
- **determiners**
- **prepositions**
- **pronouns**.

These are sometimes referred to as **structure words** because their function is to contribute to the structure of phrases, clauses, and sentences, rather than to add to their meaning content.

Words are frequently shifted from one class to another. For example, the noun *impact* is sometimes used as a verb:

The current erratic supply of diesel has **impacted** negatively on the business community …

This process is known as **conversion.**

Similarities and differences between words

For many open class words it is possible to find words of a similar meaning (**synonyms**) and words of opposite meaning (**antonyms**). Some words also have **homophones** that sound the same but are spelled differently and **homographs** that are spelled the same but have different meanings. Homographs and homophones are also referred to as **homonyms**.

Further information

The information given above is summed up in the diagram below. Each of the words in bold type has its own entry, where further information can be found.

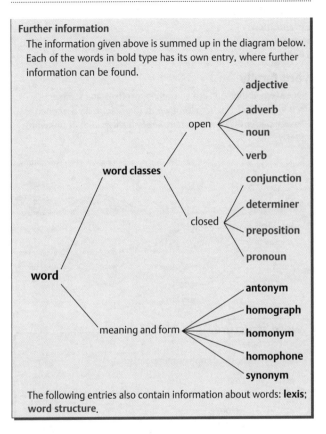

The following entries also contain information about words: **lexis**; **word structure**.

word class

Words can be grouped according to the way(s) in which they are used grammatically. The groups into which they are placed are referred to as word classes (or, in older grammatical terminology, parts of speech). The eight word classes are:

- **adjectives**
- **adverbs**
- **conjunctions**
- **determiners**
- **nouns**

W

- prepositions
- pronouns
- verbs.

word family

One **stem** combined with a variety of **prefixes** and **suffixes** produces a group or 'family' of words (more formally described as a 'lexical pattern'). Thus the stem *weight* is the parent of this word family:

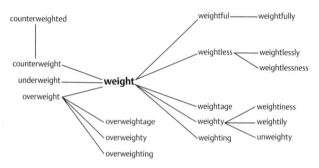

word structure

Words can consist of one or more parts:

PREFIX	STEM/BASE	SUFFIX
	weight	
	weight	less
counter	weight	
counter	weight	ed

The ways in which these parts are combined to form words constitute the structure of those words. All the words built up on the stem *weight* constitute a **word family**.

Words can also be formed by the combination of two existing words into a **compound word**:

  bookseller   paper-knife   ice cream

See also: **base**; **derivational morphology**; **diminutive**; **root**; **syllable**.

w

would

A **modal auxiliary verb** used to refer to a range of possibilities in the future. For example:

I think she **would** feel left out.

If Catherine wanted something, I **would** give it to her.

The effect of using *would* instead of *will* can be seen when we make the substitution:

I think she **will** feel left out.

If Catherine wants something, I **will** give it to her.

The versions using *will* are more open: the event may or may not happen. The sentences using *would* seem less open and less likely, although the event is still theoretically possible.

Other uses of *would* are:

■ habitual actions in the past:

Often she **would** go to Nairobi or the coast for a break.

■ actions that are regarded as typical:

He **would** do that, wouldn't he?

Would is often followed by *have*, which turns it into a past tense:

I don't suppose they **would have** liked it.

In speech this is often shortened to *would've*, which is sometimes confused with *would of*:

Anywhere else **would of** been fine. ✗

This should be:

Anywhere else **would have** been fine. ✓

yes/no question

A question that is framed in such a way that the only possible answers are 'yes', 'no', or 'I don't know'. In questions of this type the form of the verb and the word order are changed:

She	won	first prize.
subject	**verb**	**object**
	↓		
Did	she	win	first prize?
auxiliary verb	**subject**	**main verb**	**object**

zero relative

Relative clauses are often introduced by a **relative pronoun**:

He stopped in front of Siri, **who** was still lying down on the ground.

It must have something to do with a book **that** I am reading.

In sentences like the second example, we can miss out the relative pronoun:

It must have something to do with a book I am reading.

When this happens, it is said that the relative clause is introduced by a zero relative.

In **standard English** the zero relative can only function as the object of the relative clause. So in the example above you can't remove *who*:

He stopped in front of Siri, was still lying down on the ground. ✗

This non-standard use of a zero relative as the subject of a relative clause is rare:

When you live by yourself in a house you rarely leave **and is even more rarely visited**, it's essential that you don't lose track of the time. ✗

Here there are two relative clauses modifying *house*:

you rarely leave

is even more rarely visited

Omitting *which* or *that* from the beginning of the second makes the sentence read oddly. It would be better recast:

When you live by yourself in a house **that** you rarely leave and **that** is even more rarely visited, it's essential that you don't lose track of the time.